The KIDS' STUFF™ Book of

MATH

For The Primary Grades

$\frac{3}{4} \times 2 = x$

by Marjorie Frank

illustrated by Kathleen Bullock

Incentive Publications, Inc.
Nashville, Tennessee

Illustrated by Kathleen Bullock
Cover by Susan Eaddy
Edited by Sally Sharpe

ISBN 0-86530-040-2

TABLE OF CONTENTS

MEASUREMENT

TIME & MONEY

WELCOME TO PRIMARY MATH...

The world of the primary student is full of math. Math can be found on the playground, in the gymnasium, in the kitchen, around the house, in the backyard, and even at a piano lesson. Every day there are things to be measured, calculated or deciphered with mathematical skills. Abilities mushroom quickly in the early years, and some of the most exciting adventures for young minds are those that math activities provide.

THE KIDS' STUFF™ BOOK OF MATH FOR THE PRIMARY GRADES was created just for students of this age. Its purpose is to capture the interest and imaginations of young learners and to spark the growth of math skills needed for successful living.

This book was also created for you, the primary teacher. Each chapter division contains teacher pages (lessons that require very little advance preparation) and reproducible student pages (ready-to-use activities which require minimal teacher direction). For your convenience, every activity is grouped according to a major math area of the primary math curriculum. In addition, every page is clearly labeled with the emphasized skill.

Furthermore, a generous appendix has been included especially for the busy primary teacher (Math Tools and Treasures). This section has everything you need for teaching math — formulas, symbols, measurement tables and the most complete glossary of math terms you've ever seen!

You'll find this book to be a handy tool to have at your finger tips. There are enough extra investigations and challenges to supplement your basic math program all year long!

Marjorie Frank

HOW TO USE THIS BOOK . . .

THE KIDS' STUFF™ BOOK OF MATH FOR THE PRIMARY GRADES is loaded with the kinds of "extras" that enrich basic primary math programs. This book also contains thoroughly outlined lessons. These lessons introduce and reinforce solid, basic skills. You'll find plenty of ideas for teaching a concept, presenting a unit, or motivating involvement in a new area of math. On some days, this resource will be a wonderful break from the textbook. On other days it will be the textbook's best companion!

Begin by familiarizing yourself with the chapter contents. In the table of contents, each activity is labeled by skill. When you are in need of a lesson plan or a math exercise for your students, simply choose one suited to the skill you are studying.

The symbol identifies the teacher pages. Each of these pages outlines a plan for you to follow in presenting a teacher-directed math activity to the class. Quite often a student page accompanies a teacher page so that the concept may be strengthened by student practice.

The student pages, labeled with a symbol, invite students to investigate a problem or complete an interesting task. These are not "busywork" but are work sheets intended to be used with teacher direction — often as an integral part of a lesson you present. Once underway, however, the student pages may be completed on an individual basis with little teacher involvement.

The appendix, Math Tools and Treasures, may be used as a reference section for you and your students. You will find the many tables, formulas, and listings helpful for individual student use.

At the end of this book is an answer section which includes solutions to "tricky" problems. Of course, activities having a variety of possible answers are not included in this section.

- You have permission to reproduce pages labeled as student pages and pages included in the Math Tools and Treasures appendix.

Numeration &
Number Concepts

Count Before You Eat

Preparation:
- You will need small paper cups, five to seven mixing bowls, and small, edible items such as:

raisins	seeds	corn nuts
nuts	Cheerios	pretzels
corn chips	puffed cereal	dried fruit

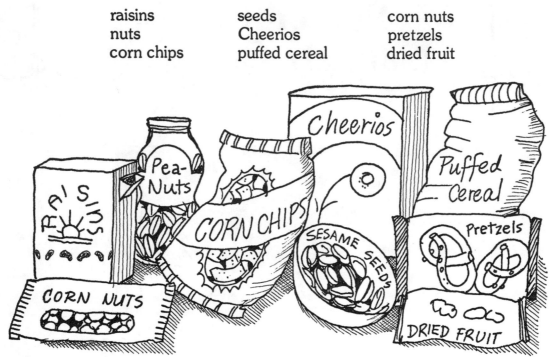

Use:
1) Make sure that all students have clean hands.
2) Divide the class into five to seven small groups. Give each group several empty paper cups.
3) Give each group a bowl of food. Direct each group to sort the items into the paper cups, counting as they do so.
4) When all of the items have been counted, the students may eat them!

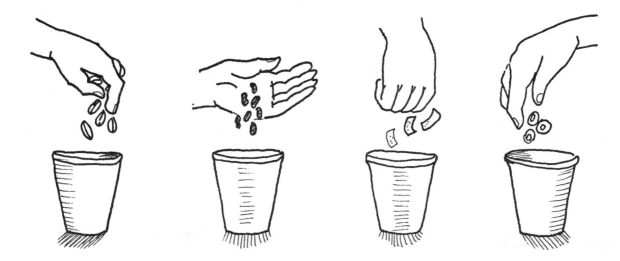

Name _____

Number Safari

Find the numbers listed below hiding in the picture.
Use a crayon to color each number as you find it.

ten	eight	fifteen	zero
four	eleven	twenty-seven	forty
three	one hundred	twelve	
nine	fifty	six	

Student Page

Body Statistics

Preparation:
- You will need a classroom full of kids and a watch or clock with a second hand for this activity.

Use:

1) Tell the students that you are going to time them for half a minute and that you want them to count how many times they swallow before time is up.

2) Next, ask the class to be very quiet. Time them to see how long they can be quiet without anyone giggling.

3) Hand out copies of the student page "Quick Counting" (page 15). Work through the items together, giving the students time to count each one. In some cases, you'll need to time the students. In other cases, the students will need to time each other.

4) Students can count other "body statistics" and add the findings to the student sheets.

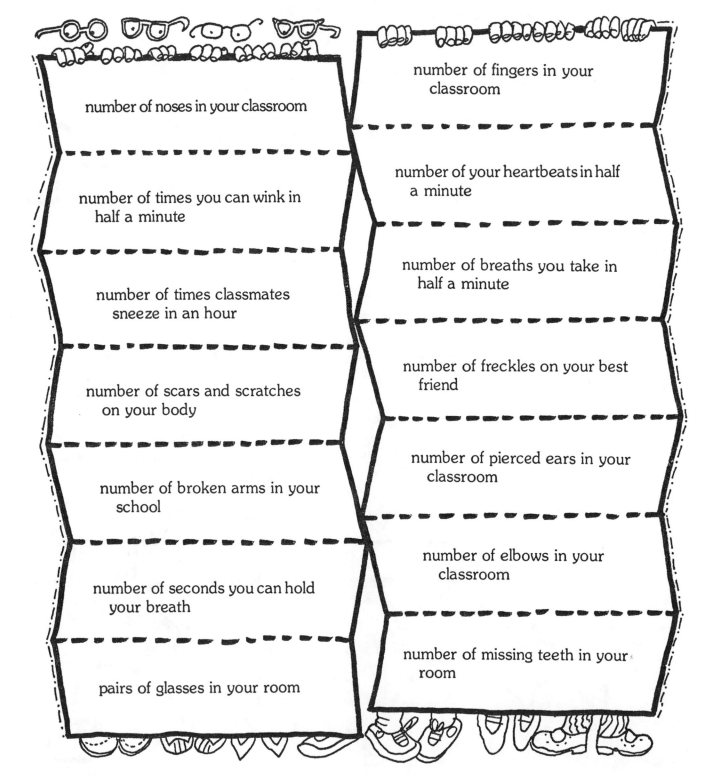

Quick Counting

Count these!

number of noses in your classroom

number of times you can wink in half a minute

number of times classmates sneeze in an hour

number of scars and scratches on your body

number of broken arms in your school

number of seconds you can hold your breath

pairs of glasses in your room

number of fingers in your classroom

number of your heartbeats in half a minute

number of breaths you take in half a minute

number of freckles on your best friend

number of pierced ears in your classroom

number of elbows in your classroom

number of missing teeth in your room

Name _____

Skipping Allowed

These skippers are skip counting!
Complete the counting for each individual.

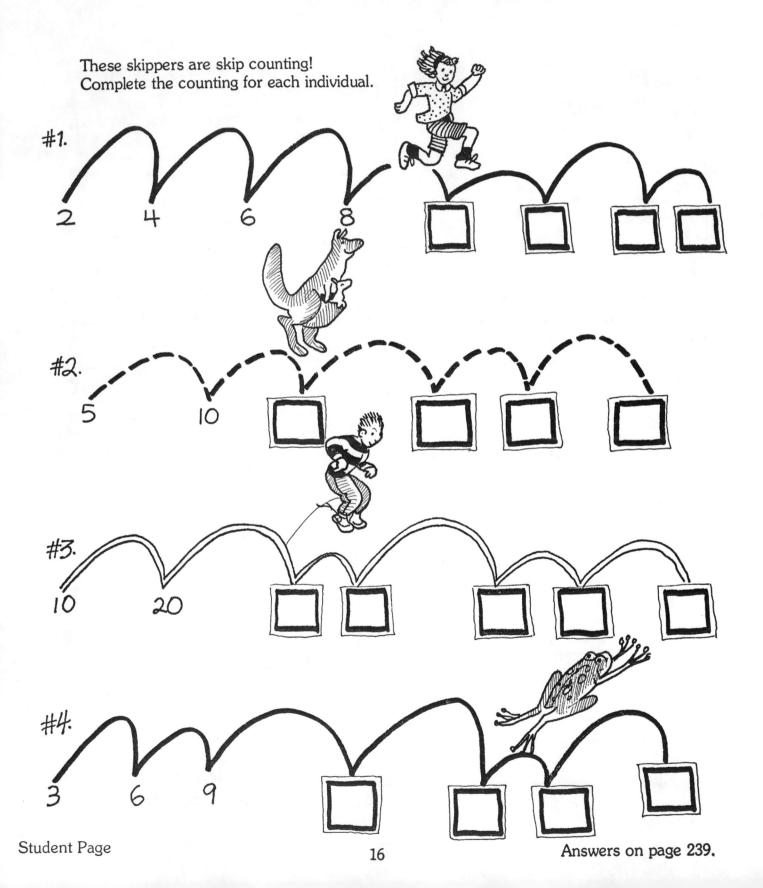

#1.

2   4   6   8   ☐   ☐   ☐   ☐

#2.

5   10   ☐   ☐   ☐   ☐

#3.

10   20   ☐   ☐   ☐   ☐   ☐

#4.

3   6   9   ☐   ☐   ☐   ☐

Name _____

It's Abominable!

Do you know what abominable means? It means awful or unpleasant.

This abominable snowman has made an abominable mess of these numbers!

Cut out the snowballs below. Correct the wrong number matches made by the abominable snowman by pasting the correct snowball above the corresponding number word.

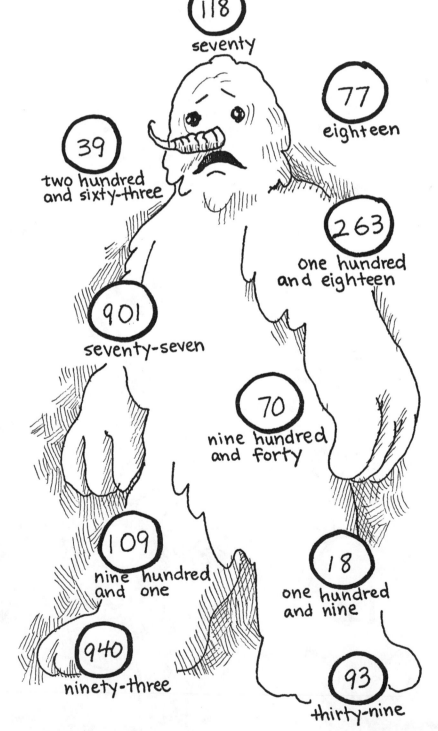

39

seventy

77

eighteen

39
two hundred and sixty-three

263
one hundred and eighteen

901
seventy-seven

70
nine hundred and forty

109
nine hundred and one

18
one hundred and nine

940
ninety-three

93
thirty-nine

39 77 263 901 70 109 18 940 93 118

Student Page

Whose T-Shirt?

These bears are looking for their shirts. Find the right shirt for each bear on page 19.

Numeration & Number Concepts
Naming Numbers

Name _____

Color and cut out the shirts. Glue each shirt on the right bear on page 18.

one thousand

ninety-five

twelve

twenty-two

forty

six hundred

sixty-six

one hundred

seventy-three

Student Page

Numbers In Bloom

Preparation:

- Cut large circles out of bright colors of construction paper. Print a number word on each circle in large letters.
- Have scissors, glue, and plenty of colored paper available for students to use in making flowers.

Use:

1) Discuss the idea that a number can have more than one name. Work together to think of several names for a number. Write the names on the board.

2) Give each student a circle with a number word written on it. Tell the students that the circles are the centers of flowers. Give the students scissors, glue, and paper. Instruct them to make several petals, and to write on each petal a way to name the number.

3) As students make petals and glue them to circles to make flowers, circulate around the room to help students think of different ways to name their numbers.

4) Display the finished flowers in a bulletin board garden.

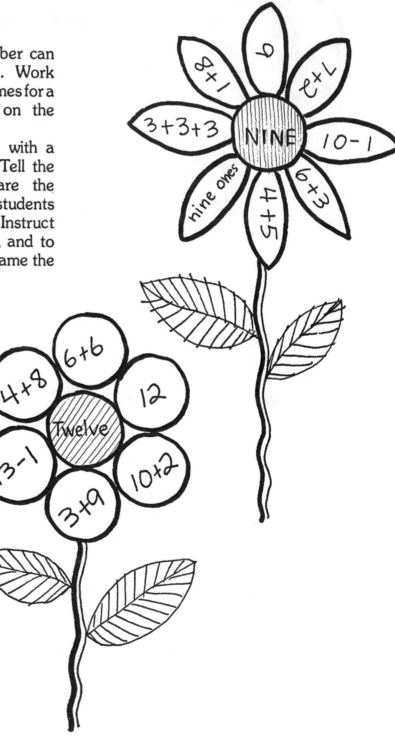

The Trains Explain

Preparation:
- You will need colored construction paper, scissors, hole punches, and yarn.
- Make a train engine for each student and write three or more digit numerals on each engine. (You may want to have students make these.)
- Make one number train as an example for the students.

Use:
1) Explain expanded notation to the students by showing them a train engine with a numeral written on it. Tape the engine to the board. Then, take one digit at a time and add a car to the train which explains that digit. (See the example.)
2) Give each student an engine, scissors, and paper. Ask the student to make a car for each digit in the numeral on the engine. Supervise as students write on each car in pencil.
3) When a student is sure the cars are labeled correctly, he or she may go over the numbers with a marker. Then the student may punch a hole in the front and back of each car (front only for the caboose) and connect the cars with yarn ties.

Teacher Page

Do-It-Yourself Roman Numerals

Preparation:
- You will need a generous supply of toothpicks, poster board, scissors, and glue.

Use:
1) Give each student a piece of poster board at least 12 x 18 inches, a handful of toothpicks, and glue.
2) Explain the Roman numeral system to the class. After doing so, let the students actually make the numerals to represent the following numbers. They may do this by gluing toothpicks to poster board to make individual charts.

Include:

1	5	10	50
100	500	1000	4
9	40		

3) Students may use their charts as guides for completing the student page "Just Like The Romans" (page 23).

I (1)   V (5)   IV (4)   X (10)

IX (9)   L (50)   XL (40)

C (100)   D (500)   M (1000)

Name _____

Just Like The Romans

Use your Roman numeral chart to help you write the "numbers" below.

your age

your birthday

your grade

the answer to ten minus one

number of teachers in
your school

today's date

number of students
in your class

number of students in
your school

Write the Arabic numerals for the Roman numerals below.

1. VIII _____
2. MD _____
3. LXI _____

4. CIII _____
5. CLVII _____
6. XIX _____

7. XXXIX _____
8. DLXXX _____
9. CXI _____

Getting To Know Large Numbers

Preparation:

- Gather a supply of drawing paper and crayons or markers.
- Make one copy of the following page.

Use:

Students are fascinated with large numbers. At the same time, students often have trouble reading and understanding them. Connecting large numbers to some actual item, place, or situation helps to make them more concrete. (See page 25.)

1) Cut apart the items on the following page. Give one to each student.
2) Pass out drawing paper and crayons or markers. Each student should use a dark crayon to print the large number in big numerals across the top of the paper. Tell each student to draw a large picture to go with the large number item they've received.
3) Have the students glue or staple the item slips to the bottom corners of their drawings. Take turns showing drawings and reading the numbers together as a class.

Distance to the moon 238,857 miles	Largest island — Greenland 840,000 sq miles
Deepest spot in the Pacific 35,840 feet	World's highest mountain — Mt. Everest 29,028 feet
Longest waterfalls — Angel Falls 3212 feet	Deepest lake — Lake Baykal 5315 feet
Largest continent — Asia 17,250 sq miles	Interior temperature of the sun 35,000,000° F
Distance to the sun 92,900,000 miles	Largest desert — Sahara 3,500,000 sq miles
Largest lake — Caspian Sea 143,244 sq miles	Length of equator (approximation) 24,902 miles
Largest ocean — Pacific 64,186,300 sq miles	Number of U.S. homes with televisions (Jan. 1, 1986) 85,590,000
People in the world who speak English (1986) 420,000,000	Bound volumes of books in Philadelphia's public libraries in 1985 3,038,638
Enrollment in public schools in 1984 39,304,541	Total take-offs and landings in the Chicago O'Hare International Airport in 1985 768,079
Eggs produced in Nebraska in 1982 809,000,000	Beef eaten in the U.S. in 1985 25,342,000 pounds
Speed of light 186,282 statute miles per second	Diameter of Jupiter (the largest planet) 88,000 miles
Babies born in the U.S. in 1984 3,697,000	Number of patients admitted to U.S. hospitals in 1983 39,000,000
Longest river — Amazon 4000 miles	Population of Toledo, Ohio in 1980 354,635
U.S. Army Military Personnel on Active Duty in 1986 776,244	Students at Florida State University in 1985-86 20,544

Inside-Out Numbers

Preparation:
- Write the number words for large numbers (three digits or more) on small slips of paper. Fold each paper and place it inside a balloon. As you place a paper in a balloon, blow up the balloon and write the numeral on the outside with a permanent marker.

Use:

1) Show the balloons to the students. Tell the students that the "names" of the numerals are hiding inside the balloons.

2) Give each student a balloon. Have each student copy his or her number on paper and write out the number in words as it should read.

3) Let the students burst their balloons and read the number words inside to check themselves.

23,017

3,000,003

8264

566,066

Take Off Your Shoes

Preparation:
- Cut five pieces of rope or heavy yarn, each approximately six feet long.
- For this activity you will need an open area where students can sit in a circle.

Use:
1) Seat the students in a large circle. Have each student take off one shoe and place it in the center of the circle.
2) Make one or more large circles with the yarn pieces. Use these circles to contain sets that the students create. Give directions such as:

   Make a set of the shoes with laces.
   Make a set of the shoes with rubber soles.
   Make a set of white shoes.

3) Have students form equivalent sets. Make two or three yarn circles and instruct the students to put the same number of shoes in each set.
4) The students may also practice writing numerals to match the sets. Have individuals go to the board and write numerals to answer questions such as:

   How many are in the set of red shoes?
   How many are in the set of shoes with hard soles?
   How many are in the set of new shoes?

Teacher Page

All Decked Out

Preparation:
- Gather a collection of small objects such as paper clips, counting blocks, buttons, etc. You will also need a few decks of playing cards and several small paper cups.

Use:
1) Give each student a paper cup with several small objects inside it.
2) Pass out several playing cards to each student.
3) Have each student select one card at a time. Instruct each student to create a set of objects to match the number on the card. If the objects are small enough, the students may actually match the objects to the symbols on the playing cards by placing the objects on top of the symbols.
4) Students may trade cards with one another for more practice in making and matching sets.

Name _____

Lasso A Set

Cowgirl Cathy
needs some help!

1

20 2 5 12

25 80

10

4

6 87

31 26 40

8

30 75 100

63 50 6

60 14 49

99

15

70 3

Draw a lasso around a set of five numbers.
Color the set blue.

Lasso a set of ten numbers and color it green.

Lasso a set of seven numbers and color it yellow.

Lasso an empty set and color it pink.

Lasso a set of three numbers and color it orange.

13 38 90

Student Page

Number Soup

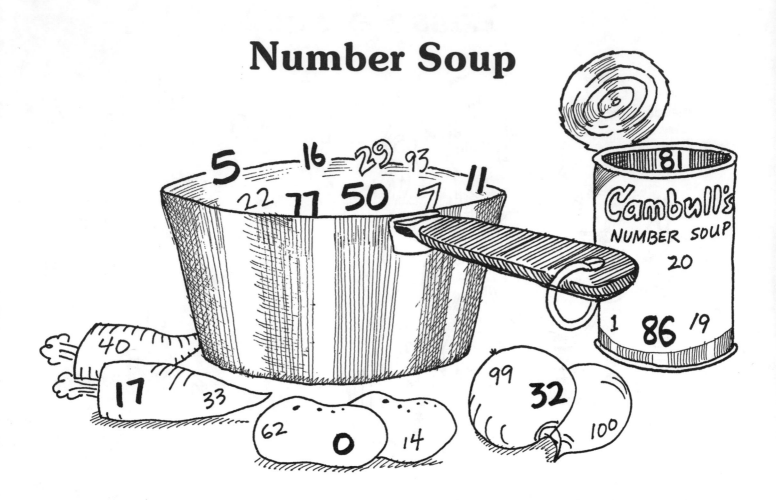

Preparation:
- Make a bulletin board display of a large pot of soup full of numbers (see the illustration). Students may help with this by making vegetables with numbers on them for the soup.

Use:
1) Ask the students to see how many numbers they can find in the soup. Read the numbers aloud as the students "find" them.
2) Let the students work in small groups to put all of the numbers in order from smallest to largest.
3) Compare the number soup sequences when each group is finished.
4) For more sequencing practice, give each student a copy of the student page "Mix-Up To Fix Up" (page 31).

Mix-Up To Fix Up

These friends are not in the right order. Cut the squares apart on the dotted lines and line them up in the right order. Then tape the squares together to make one long line.

Student Page

Know Your Places

Preparation:

- Make copies of the student page "Whooo Am I?" (page 33) for the students.
- Have on hand the following things: a large shopping bag, brown and yellow construction paper, scissors, glue, and markers.

Use:

1) Let the students enjoy completing the "Whooo Am I?" student page. If necessary, work as a group on this page.

2) Use construction paper to make large owls. Encourage students to be creative in designing their owls.

3) After the students have completed their owls and have written their names on the backs, collect the owls and write three or four-digit numerals on the fronts with a marker. (Use larger numerals if appropriate for student level.) Put the owls into a shopping bag.

4) Tell the students that you are going to play a "Whooo Am I?" game. Begin by choosing an owl from the bag and giving clues for the number. For example:

   I am 4 thousands and 3 tens. Whooo am I?

   (That reads 4030.)

5) Let the students take turns choosing owls and giving clues.

Name _____

Whooo Am I?

Write the correct number on each owl's tummy.

1) I am: 5 hundreds
8 tens
6 ones
Whooo am I?

2) I am: 1 hundred
9 tens
0 ones
Whooo am I?

3) I am: 2 hundreds
0 tens
8 ones
Whooo am I?

4) I am: 5 hundreds
8 tens
3 ones
Whooo am I?

5) I am: 8 hundreds
6 tens
3 ones
Whooo am I?

6) I am: 9 hundreds
6 tens
0 ones
Whooo am I?

7) I am: 2 hundreds
4 tens
7 ones
Whooo am I?

8) I am: 9 hundreds
0 tens
0 ones
Whooo am I?

9) I am: 9 hundreds
2 tens
9 ones
Whooo am I?

Answers on page 239.

33

Student Page

Hang It!

Preparation:
- String a clothesline or wire from one corner of the classroom to the opposite corner.
- You will need a supply of clip-type clothespins, drawing paper, construction paper, crayons, markers, scissors, and glue.

Use:
1) Ask the students to draw and cut out things to hang on the clothesline such as socks, pants, shirts, hats, blankets, or towels. They might want to add funny things such as a teddy bear, a wig, a bearskin rug, etc.
2) Hang the completed items on the clothesline and use the "line-up" for practice with ordinal numbers by asking and directing such things as:

Which item is fourth in the line-up?
Hang the catcher's mit to be the eleventh item in the line-up.
What place does the green sock hold?
Which item is sixth from the end?

Name _____

Which Web?

Decide if the number on each spider is odd or even.
Cut out the spiders along the dotted lines and glue each one on the correct web.

35   Student Page

Star Struck

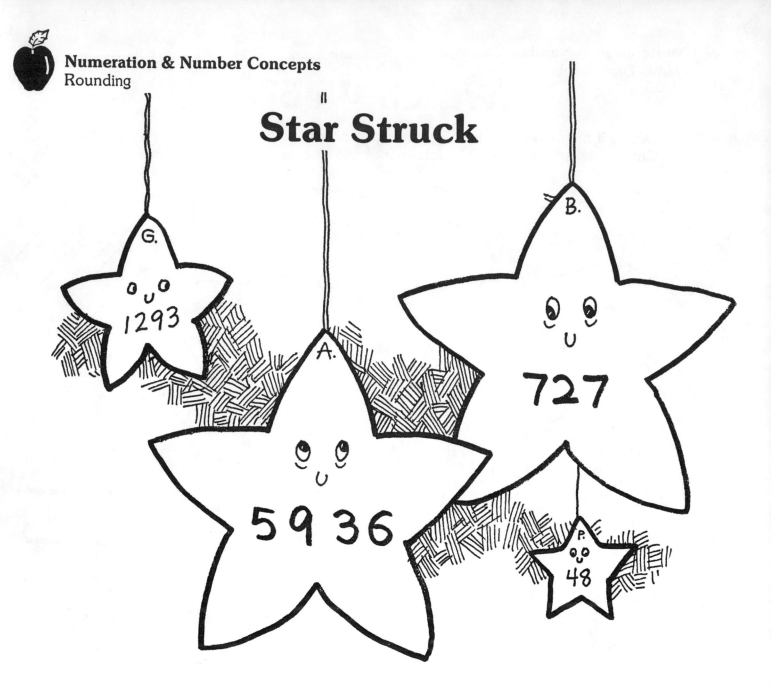

Preparation:

- Make approximately 20 stars using yellow or white poster board. (You may want to cover the stars with foil for a shiny look.) Write a number of two to four digits on each star. Label the stars with letters beginning with "A."
- Hang the stars from the ceiling with string.

Use:

1) Ask the students to round the numbers on the stars to the nearest 10. Point out that each star is labeled with a letter to help the students identify the stars when writing the answers.

2) Ask the students to begin again, rounding each number to the nearest 100. Later, the students may round to the nearest 1000.

3) Hand out copies of the student page "Rounding Robots" (page 37) for more practice in rounding.

Rounding Robots

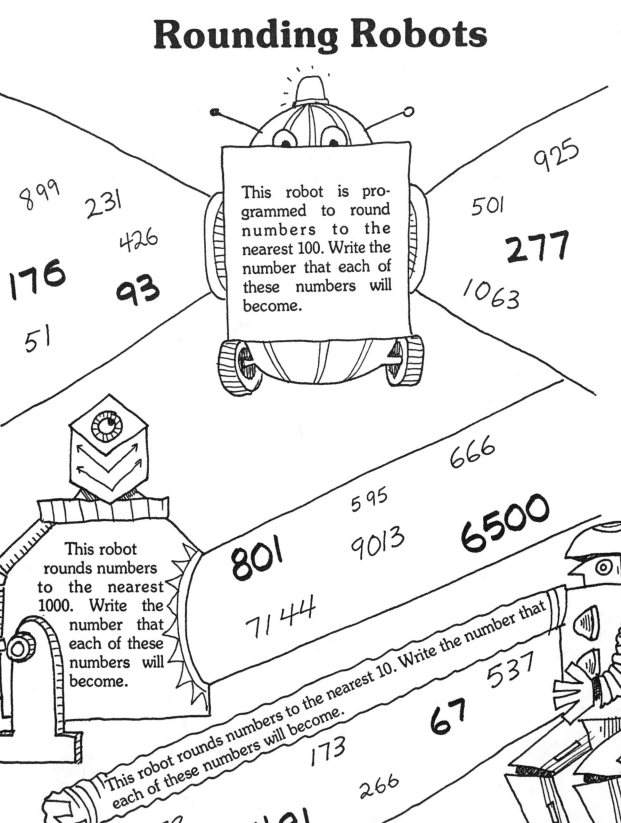

899   231
426
176   93
51

This robot is programmed to round numbers to the nearest 100. Write the number that each of these numbers will become.

925
501
277
1063

This robot rounds numbers to the nearest 1000. Write the number that each of these numbers will become.

801   595   666
9013   6500
7144

This robot rounds numbers to the nearest 10. Write the number that each of these numbers will become.

537
67
173
266
88   491

37

People Math

Preparation:
- Make a paper plate "necklace" for each student by stringing yarn through two holes in a paper plate. Make the necklace long enough to hang around a child's neck.
- Write one of the following symbols on each of two plates: $<$, $>$.
- Write a one or two-digit numeral on each of the other plates.

Use:
1) Give a plate necklace to each student.
2) Use the students to form number sentences which express inequalities. Begin by asking two students to come to the front of the room. Have the class decide which symbol should go between the numbers ($<$ or $>$).

Hop-A-Problem

Preparation:

- Make a "math-mat" such as the one shown below by writing numbers, the addition sign, the subtraction sign, and the equals sign on an old shower curtain or piece of vinyl with a permanent marker.

Use:

1) Lay the math-mat on a carpet, or tape each corner of the mat to a hard floor.
2) Show the students how the mat can be used to "hop" problems. For example:

Have a student "hop" the equation (5 + 6). The student hops from the five to the addition sign, from there to the six, from there to the equals sign, and from there to the eleven.

3) The mat can be used by individuals, pairs, or groups of students to practice addition and subtraction facts.

Name _____

Don't Let Any Get Away

This furry critter is fishing for missing addends. Which fish will he catch on each hook?

Cut out the fish and glue each one on the right hook.

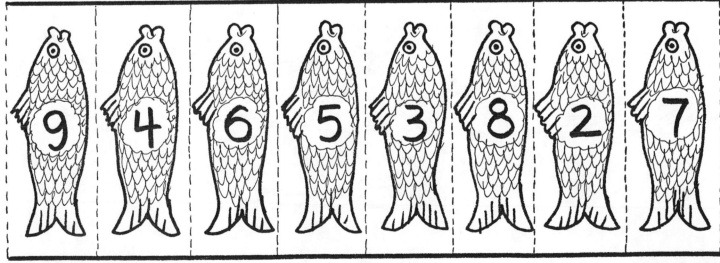

41

Math On A Shoestring

Preparation:
- Gather the following:
  - a long shoestring for each student (tie a fat knot at one end of each shoestring)
  - a supply of beads, noodles, or pasta with holes (one full plastic bag for each student)

Use:

1) Use the shoestrings and noodles as portable number lines. Place problems such as those below on the board and have students work them on their number lines. Ask the students to hold up their strings to show their answers.

$$4 + 5 = \underline{\hspace{1cm}} \qquad\qquad 7 + \underline{\hspace{1cm}} = 11$$
$$3 + \underline{\hspace{1cm}} = 8 \qquad\qquad \underline{\hspace{1cm}} + 6 = 6$$

2) Use the shoestring number lines for subtraction problems, too.

$$12 - 5 = \underline{\hspace{1cm}} \qquad\qquad 10 - \underline{\hspace{1cm}} = 3$$
$$4 - \underline{\hspace{1cm}} = 4 \qquad\qquad 15 - \underline{\hspace{1cm}} = 9$$

You will be able to see at a glance if students are solving problems correctly.

3) After you've practiced working problems as a class, give the students copies of the student page "String-A-Problem" (page 43) to work on their own.

Name _____

String-A-Problem

Shoestrings can be used for more than just tying shoes!

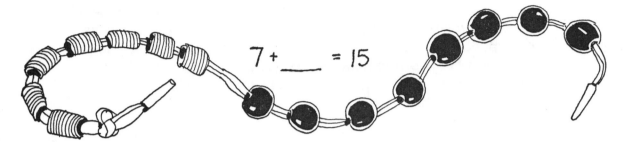

$7 +$ ___ $= 15$

Use your shoestring and noodles to find the missing numbers in these addition problems.

$3 + 6 =$ _____

$8 + 2 =$ _____

$1 +$ _____ $= 9$

$4 + 7 =$ _____

$0 + 10 =$ _____

$5 +$ _____ $= 8$

$7 + 7 =$ _____

$9 +$ _____ $= 18$

You can do shoestring subtraction, too.

$12 - 8 =$ ___

Find the missing numbers in these subtraction problems by using your shoestring and noodles.

$9 - 4 =$ _____

$12 -$ _____ $= 5$

$8 -$ _____ $= 8$

$15 - 5 =$ _____

$10 - 10 =$ _____

$9 -$ _____ $= 6$

$7 - 4 =$ _____

$11 - 3 =$ _____

43

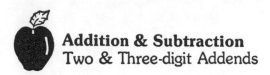
Crack The Code

Preparation:

- Prepare a special message for your students using the answers of addition and subtraction problems. Make a code chart which gives the corresponding letter for each answer. In the example below, the message is "Popcorn party at two o'clock."
- Write addition and/or subtraction problems on a sheet of paper and duplicate it for the class.

72	59	66	119	45	88	10
+83	+101	+89	+300	+115	+99	+90

103	416	123	37	111	420	182
+52	+23	+64	+200	+222	+19	+55

200	65	20	-80	'310	11	90	250	10
+37	+55	+140	+80	+109	+99	+70	+169	+33

Use:

1) Tell the students that you have written a secret message for them in code. They must crack the code to find out what the message is.
2) Write the code on the board so that everyone can see it.

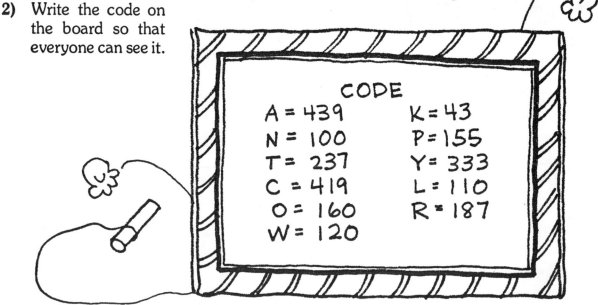

CODE

A = 439   K = 43
N = 100   P = 155
T = 237   Y = 333
C = 419   L = 110
O = 160   R = 187
W = 120

Name _____

Sports Shop Search

Each of these problems has a missing addend. Each missing addend is hidden somewhere in this sports shop. Find and circle each missing addend and then write it in the corresponding blank.

A. $7 + \underline{\hspace{1cm}} = 10$
B. $2 + \underline{\hspace{1cm}} = 14$
C. $18 - 7 = \underline{\hspace{1cm}}$

D. $\underline{\hspace{1cm}} + 6 = 13$
E. $\underline{\hspace{1cm}} + 10 = 15$
F. $17 - 9 = \underline{\hspace{1cm}}$

G. $8 + \underline{\hspace{1cm}} = 14$
H. $7 + \underline{\hspace{1cm}} = 17$
I. $9 - 5 = \underline{\hspace{1cm}}$

Student Page

The Amazing Zero

Preparation:
- Make a poster board square (about 9" x 9") for each student. Draw lines on each square dividing it into three rows of three squares (as shown).

Use:
1) Give each student a square. Ask the student to use a crayon to write a zero in the center square. Then, ask the student to write a number (0-9) in each of the other squares. Explain that each row must have at least one zero in it.
2) Ask the students to write and solve an addition problem for each row. Tell the students to pay special attention to the way that the zero affects the sum.
3) Explain the term identity element to the class.

Addition & Subtraction
Column Addition

Name _____

Sum Birthday!

Find out the birthdays of ten of your classmates. Write the birthdays in the column below by following these instructions:

Write the number of the month in the first two squares. (Write January - 01, July - 07, November - 11, etc.)

Write the number of the day in the last two squares. (For days 1-9, write a zero in front of the number.)

Birthday

MONTH		DAY	
1.			
2.			
3.			
4.			
5.			
6.			
7.			
8.			
9.			
10.			

Now add all of the numbers to solve one long addition problem!

Do this activity again with another list of ten numbers — ages, shoe sizes, or heights in inches.

Read It Backwards

Preparation:
- Write the following on the board:

    7227,   level,   too hot to hoot

Use:

1) Ask the students if they can tell what the three things above have in common.

2) When the students discover that each reads the same forwards as backwards, tell the students that such words or numbers are called palindromes.

3) Explain that any number can be made into a palindrome by using simple addition. Show the students how to do this.

Write a number.

Write the reverse of the number and then add.

$$\begin{array}{r} 824 \\ +\ 428 \\ \hline 1252 \end{array}$$

Write the answer backwards and then add the two.

Continue writing the answers backwards and then adding. Sooner or later you will get a palindrome.

$$\begin{array}{r} 1252 \\ +2521 \\ \hline 3773 \end{array}$$

(Note: Sometimes it takes a lot of adding!)

I'M TOO HOT TO HOOT!

Name _____

Eight Arms Come In Handy

Work the addition and subtraction problems on each of the octopus' arms. Write the answers at the ends of the arms.

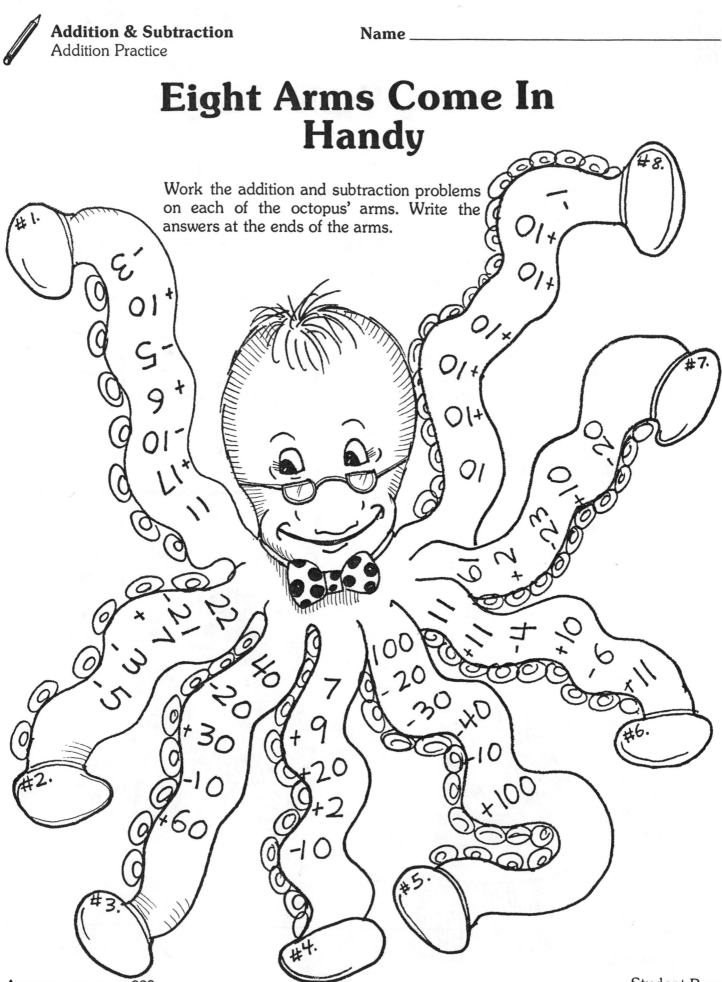

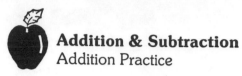

Addition Works Magic

Preparation:

- Draw the magic square shown below on the chalkboard so that all of the students may see it.

Use:

1) Tell the students that there is something magic about this square and that they can discover what it is by using addition.

2) Suggest that the students add each column horizontally, vertically, and diagonally. The students should discover that all of the sums are the same.

3) Tell the students that they will have a chance to try other magic squares. Give each student a copy of the student page "Magical Squares" (page 51) and help them complete the squares.

4) You may want to have the students work independently on the magic squares on the student page "More Magic" (page 52).

4	9	2
3	5	7
8	1	6

Magical Squares

1. Is this a magic square?

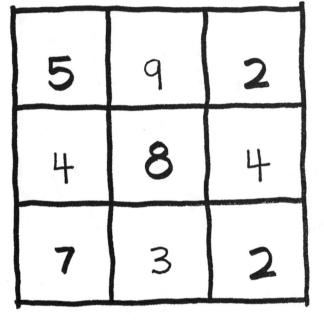

5	9	2
4	8	4
7	3	2

2. Is this a magic square?

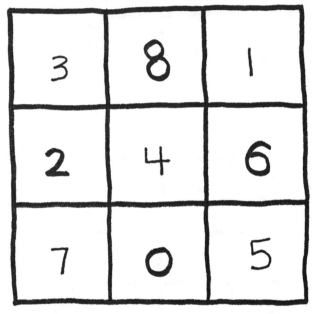

3	8	1
2	4	6
7	0	5

3. This is a magic square. Fill in the missing numbers.

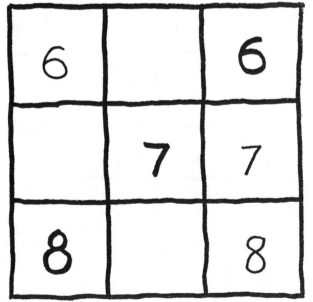

6		6
	7	7
8		8

4. Fill in the missing numbers in this magic square.

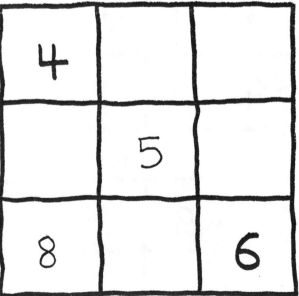

4		
	5	
8		6

More Magic

1. Finish this magic square.

5	10	3
9	2	

2. Finish this magic square.

8		10
	7	
4		6

3. Is this a magic square?

2	7	3
7	4	7
9	3	2

4. Is this a magic square?

6	0	2
1	6	1
1	2	5

5. Complete this magic square.

9		
	8	
5		7

6. Complete this magic square.

9		7
8		12
		11

Name _____

Subtraction On Wheels

This racer will begin at start with 999. Each time he comes to a flag, subtract the number on the flag from the amount he has.

The final number will tell you the racer's record time in minutes.

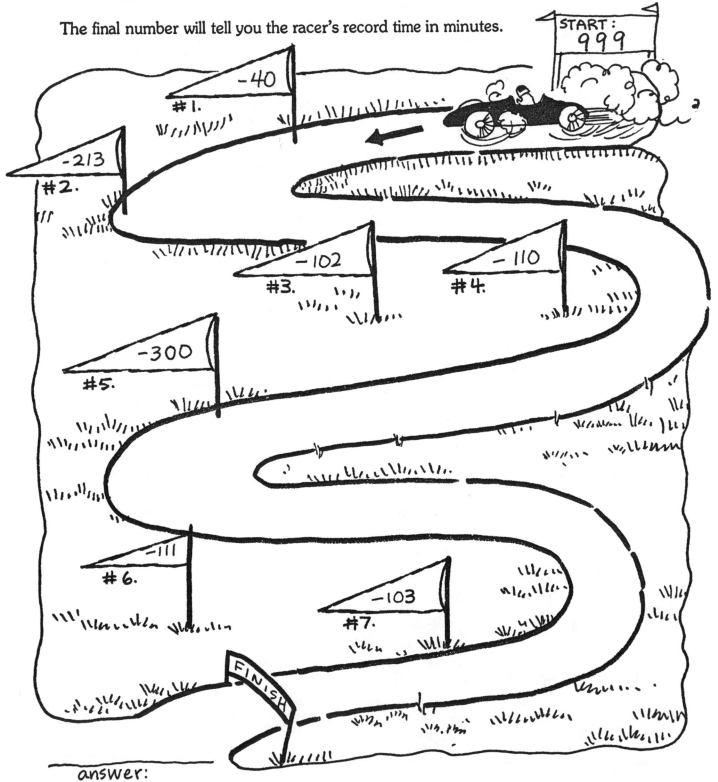

START:
999

#1. −40

#2. −213

#3. −102

#4. −110

#5. −300

#6. −111

#7. −103

FINISH

answer: _____

A Little Help From A Frog

Preparation:
- Make a desk-top number line for each student (omitting the numbers). Divide the line into 20 spaces.
- Duplicate the frog pattern on this page on stiff paper.
- You will need tape, a stapler, popsicle sticks, and crayons.

Use:
1) Give each student a number line and help the students number their lines from zero to 20.
2) Have the students tape the number lines to their desks.
3) Give each student a frog to color, name, and cut out.
4) Instruct the students to staple their frogs to popsicle sticks.
5) Show the students how their frogs can "hop" along the number line to help solve addition and subtraction problems.

Name _____

Mountain Math

These mountain climbers need help in figuring out how high the mountain that they're climbing is.

Starting with the number at the top, subtract each number from the number above it. The resulting number is the height of the mountain.

start with 12,000 feet

−2439

−100

−547

−790

−59

−65

Write your answer here:

Weight Check At The Zoo

Preparation:

- Plan to have two or three days for this activity.
- Gather paint, brushes, large mural paper, markers, scissors, encyclopedias, and black yarn.

Use:

1) Talk with the students about visits to the zoo. Make a list of animals they've seen at the zoo.

2) Have the students work in pairs or small groups to draw, paint, and cut out several zoo animals.

3) Display the animals on a wall or large bulletin board. Pin strips of yarn over the animals to create the look of a cage.

4) Help the students use encyclopedias to find the approximate weights of the zoo animals. Label the animals' weights clearly.

5) Practice reading the weights with the students and work a few problems together. For example:

    Is the weight of the elephant less than or greater than that of the seal?

6) Give each student a copy of the student page "Great and Small . . . Weigh Them All" (page 57). (If your display includes different animals, make a similar page of your own.)

Name _____

Great And Small ... Weigh Them All

300 lbs.

5 lbs.

2000 lbs.

A. Find the weight for each animal in the problems below.

Then put < or > in the empty space.

1. Zebra _____ snake.

2. Alligator _____ peacock.

3. Rhinoceros _____ turtle.

4. Hippopotamus _____ rhinoceros.

5. Monkey _____ panda.

6. Lion _____ elephant.

7. Polar bear _____ peacock.

8. Zebra _____ giraffe.

B. Write the weight of each animal in place of the animal name and then put < or > in the empty space.

600 lbs.

450 lbs.

45 lbs.

1) Turtle + monkey _____ polar bear.

2) Alligator - snake _____ turtle.

3) Giraffe _____ zebra + lion.

4) Panda - zebra _____ elephant.

100 lbs.

70 lbs.

1600 lbs.

2500 lbs.

350 lbs.

500 lbs.

8 lbs.

Words That Add Up

Preparation:
- Cut drawing paper into 18" x 6" strips.
- Make copies of the student page "Add Popcorn To Shampoo?" (page 59).

Use:
1) Work with the students to add and subtract the words and sentences on the student page. (Tell students to count the letters and then add.)
2) Practice creating similar problems as a class. For an extra challenge, try to think of words for the answers, too.
3) Let the students work individually or in pairs to make up problems of their own. The students may write the problems on the strips of paper and then trade problems with other students.

Roosevelt School   15
+ Third Grade   +10
      25

Sandy   5
+ Nelsonson   +9
    14

Monster   7
+ Mischief   +8
    15

Chocolate   9
+ Chip   +4
   13

Name _____

Add Popcorn To Shampoo?

Try adding popcorn to shampoo!

Write the number of letters in the word popcorn and then add the number of letters in the word shampoo.

The answer is 14.

Work the problems below by writing the number of letters in the first word and then adding the number of letters in the second word (and third, and fourth, etc.).

Example:

POPCORN   7
+ SHAMPOO   + 7
                          ____
                           14

1.   Easter
   + Halloween

3. Abracadabra
      + Witch
   _____

2.   pizza
   root beer
   French fries
   ice cream
   + tummy ache
   _____

4. MICKEY MOUSE
   + DONALD DUCK
   _____

5. summer
    - fall
   _____

6. Scary
   + Monster
   _____

Name _____

Smart Guessing

Nancy Numbers is trying to guess what the answers to these problems will be.

You can help her by estimating. Circle the closest estimate for each problem.

52 $+21$	A.	40	70	20	50
685 -380	B.	200	250	400	300
29 $+39$	C.	70	60	30	80
48 $+59$	D.	100	110	90	80
999 -699	E.	600	700	500	300
500 $-\ \ 7$	F.	10	110	300	500

See It Clearly

Preparation:
- Have graph paper (1 cm squares) and crayons or markers available for the students.

Use:

Graph paper is a handy tool for helping students to clearly visualize multiplication and division. One can use graph paper to show multiplication as a combination of subsets into sets, and to show division as the separation of sets into subsets.

1) Give each student a piece of graph paper. Work together to "picture" multiplication problems. Give instructions such as:

Draw a box around a set of three squares.
Do this four more times for a total of five
    sets of three squares each.
How many total squares are enclosed?
Let's write the multiplication problem.
$$3 \times 5 = 15$$

2) Try several other "problems" together. Then give the students a few problems to do individually.

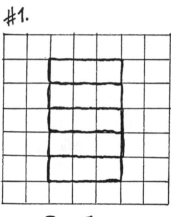

#1.

$3 \times 5 = 15$

#2.

$7 \times 3 = 21$

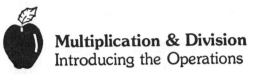

$$12 \div 3 = 4$$

3) Now give the students directions for "picturing" division problems. Give instructions such as:

Draw a rectangle to enclose 12 squares.
Draw a box around one set of three squares.
Now enclose more sets of three squares.
How many sets were you able to enclose?
Here's what we just did. We started with 12 squares and divided them into four sets with three squares each.
Let's write the division problem.

$$12 \div 3 = 4$$

4) Have the students try "picturing" a division equation with a remainder. This is a clear way to show the concept of remainders.

Teacher Page

Toss & Practice

Preparation:

- You will need a pair of dice and pencil and paper for each pair of students.

Use:

1) Let each student choose a partner.
2) Instruct each student to roll one die. Then each pair of students must multiply the two numbers they rolled and write all of the multiplication and division facts in that "family."

In the case of a 4 and a 6, the students should write:

$$4 \times 6 = 24$$

$$6 \times 4 = 24$$

$$24 \div 4 = 6$$

$$24 \div 6 = 4$$

3) For practicing facts with factors up to 12, students should roll the dice twice.

Name _____

Lost & Found

These facts have lost their answers. Find the answers in the picture. Then color each answer as directed.

Color 5 x 8 blue.
Color 8 x 7 red.
Color 8 x 6 black.
Color 9 x 4 yellow.
Color 3 x 8 white.

Color 3 x 9 green.
Color 6 x 3 orange.
Color 4 x 7 brown.
Color 8 x 9 pink.
Color 5 x 7 purple.

Student Page

Name _____

Factors On The Loose

Some factors have escaped from the circus train.

Which animal belongs where? Draw the correct animal in each train car.

1. $4 \times \square = 36$

2. $\square \times 7 = 28$

3. $3 \times \square = 18$

4. $\square \times 8 = 64$

5. $7 \times \square = 49$

66

Answers on page 239.

6. $8 \times \square = 24$

7. $7 \times \square = 35$

8. $\square \times 10 = 20$

9. $9 \times \square = 90$

Wear-A-Fact-A-Day

Preparation:
- On 6" x 6" pieces of tagboard or drawing paper, write each of the multiplication facts (with factors to 10) in the form shown below. (Do not include products.)
- Have a supply of straight pins on hand.

Use:
1) When your students are learning multiplication facts, have them wear a fact for a day or part of a day. Whenever anyone asks the question written on the fact card, the student must give the answer.
2) Switch facts daily or as often as needed.
3) Have each individual keep a record of the facts he or she knows so that the individual does not wear those facts.

On The Trail

Write each problem and then find the answer.

1) Roberta and Sam walked 13 miles each day for 6 days. How far did they hike?

2) There are 9 trails in the park. Each is about 18 miles long. How many miles of trail are there?

3) How long will it take to walk a 25 mile trail hiking 5 miles per hour?

4) John rode for 3 hours at 15 miles per hour. Julie walked 7 miles at 4 miles per hour. Who went farther?

Fast Factor Trees

Preparation:
- Make a large tree using green construction paper or poster board.
- Glue a square with the number 36 written on it near the top of the tree.

Use:
1) Tell the students that one quick and fun way to find prime factors is to use a factor tree.
2) Ask the students to name two factors whose product is 36.
3) Glue squares onto the tree to show the factors of each factor until only prime numbers are left.
4) Try several other numbers (48, 72, 24, etc). Glue the new factors on top of those you've already put on the tree.
5) Give each student a copy of the student page "Factors That Grow On Trees" (page 71) for more practice finding prime factors.

Name _____

Factors That Grow On Trees

Complete each factor tree below.

Student Page

Lattice Multiplication

Preparation:
- Make copies of the student page "A New Way To Multiply" (page 73).
- Draw a lattice (such as shown on page 73) on the chalkboard. Write 2, 6, 3 across the top and 4, 2, 7 down the right side.

Use:
1) Explain to students that lattice multiplication is another fun way to solve or check multiplication problems.
2) Use the lattice on the chalkboard to show the students how to perform lattice multiplication.

Multiply each number down the right side by each number across the top. Write each answer in the box which corresponds with the two numbers multiplied (tens digits go above the diagonal line and ones digits go below the line).

Multiply: 4 x 3
4 x 6
4 x 2
across top row.

Multiply: 2 x 3
2 x 6
2 x 2
along middle row.

Multiply: 7 x 3
7 x 6
7 x 2
along bottom row.

Add the numbers in each diagonal row beginning in the lower right-hand corner (carry the tens digit to the next diagonal row). Read the answer beginning in the upper left-hand corner (112,301).

3) Have the students multiply 263 x 427 in the customary way to check the answer. Then have the students try another problem, using the empty grid on page 73.

A New Way To Multiply

Student Page

Name _____

Mix & Match Problems

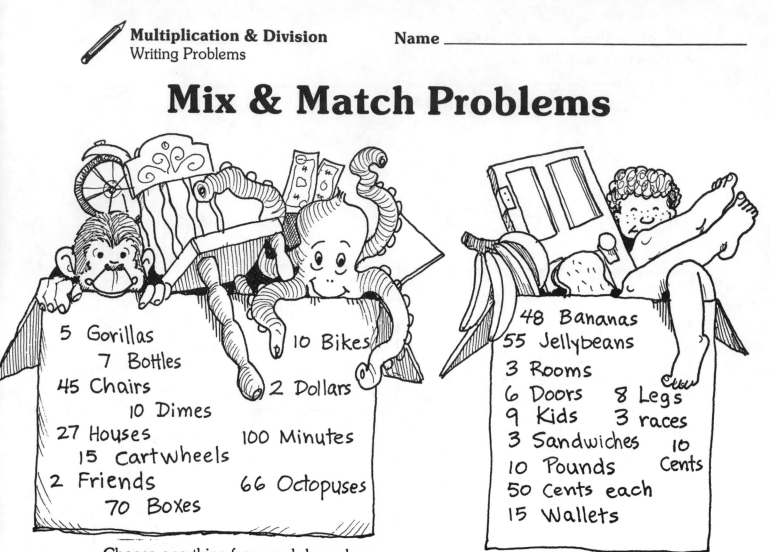

5 Gorillas
7 Bottles
45 Chairs
10 Dimes
27 Houses
15 Cartwheels
2 Friends
70 Boxes

10 Bikes
2 Dollars
100 Minutes
66 Octopuses

48 Bananas
55 Jellybeans
3 Rooms
6 Doors   8 Legs
9 Kids   3 races
3 Sandwiches   10
10 Pounds   Cents
50 Cents each
15 Wallets

Choose one thing from each box above.

Use the two items you chose to make a multiplication problem. Write the problem on line 1 below. Example:

Each of five gorillas eats 48 bananas a day. How many bananas are eaten in one day?

- -

1. _____

_____

2. _____

_____

Cut along the dotted line. Trade papers with a classmate and solve the problem you receive. Then choose two different items and use them to write a multiplication problem on line 2. Trade papers again and solve the second problem.

Name _____

12-Mile Math Marathon

How fast can you finish the marathon? Time yourself!

Solve the problems 1-12 on a separate piece of paper. Each time you find an answer, color that "mile" on the marathon course.

Try to finish all 12 miles!

41

53

50

666

75

28

1) 594 ÷ 6 = _____
2) 371 ÷ 7 = _____
3) 2664 ÷ 4 = _____
4) 225 ÷ 9 = _____

99

411

100

25

511

5) 84 ÷ 7 = _____
6) 400 ÷ 8 = _____
7) 500 ÷ 5 = _____
8) 196 ÷ 7 = _____

9) 1533 ÷ 3 = _____
10) 150 ÷ 2 = _____
11) 2466 ÷ 6 = _____
12) 205 ÷ 5 = _____

12

FINISH LINE

FINISH LINE

Don't Spit The Seeds!

Preparation:
- You'll need a slice of watermelon, a paper plate, and paper towels for each student.

Use:
1) Pass out the paper plates and paper towels. Ask the students to have paper and pencil ready.
2) Give each student a slice of watermelon. Ask the students to eat the watermelon and count the seeds as they put them on the plates.
3) Explain the concept of averaging. Tell the students you'd like to find the average number of seeds that each person has.
4) Work together to add the total number of seeds found and to divide by the number of people eating watermelon.
5) For more practice with averages, let the students work individually to complete the student page "Classroom Averages" (page 77).

Name _____

Classroom Averages

Find the averages below. (Remember: Add to find the total; divide by the number of students or classes.)

The average number of students in each class in your school.

The average number of freckles for each kid in your school.

The average number of missing teeth per student in your class.

The average number of sharp pencils per student in your class.

The average number of sisters and brothers for the students in your school.

The average number of times a student raises a hand in your class each day.

Student Page

Name _____

Dot-To-Dot What?

I like dot-to-dot puzzles

I can solve these problems easily!

Follow these directions to find out what picture is "hiding" on the next page.

1) Solve problem A. Look for the answer on page 79. Draw a line from "start" to the right answer.
2) Solve problem B and draw a line to that answer from the previous answer.
3) Continue in this way until the picture is finished.

A	2 x 20	L	90 ÷ 10
B	11 x 5	M	7 x 0
C	70 ÷ 7	N	36 x 1
D	22 ÷ 11	O	85 ÷ 1
E	9 x 10	P	12 ÷ 3
F	40 ÷ 2	Q	10 x 10
G	3 x 100	R	25 ÷ 5
H	14 x 1	S	126 ÷ 6
I	35 ÷ 5	T	7 x 11
J	25 x 2	U	61 x 1
K	16 x 3		

Multiplication & Division
Solving Problems

Name _____

Solve the problems on page 78 to connect the dots below.
Color the picture.

How's Your Divisibility Ability?

If a number is divisible by 2, then 2 is a factor of the number. That means the number can be evenly divided by 2.

You can tell if a number is divisible by 2 just by looking at the number. Here are some divisibility rules to remember.

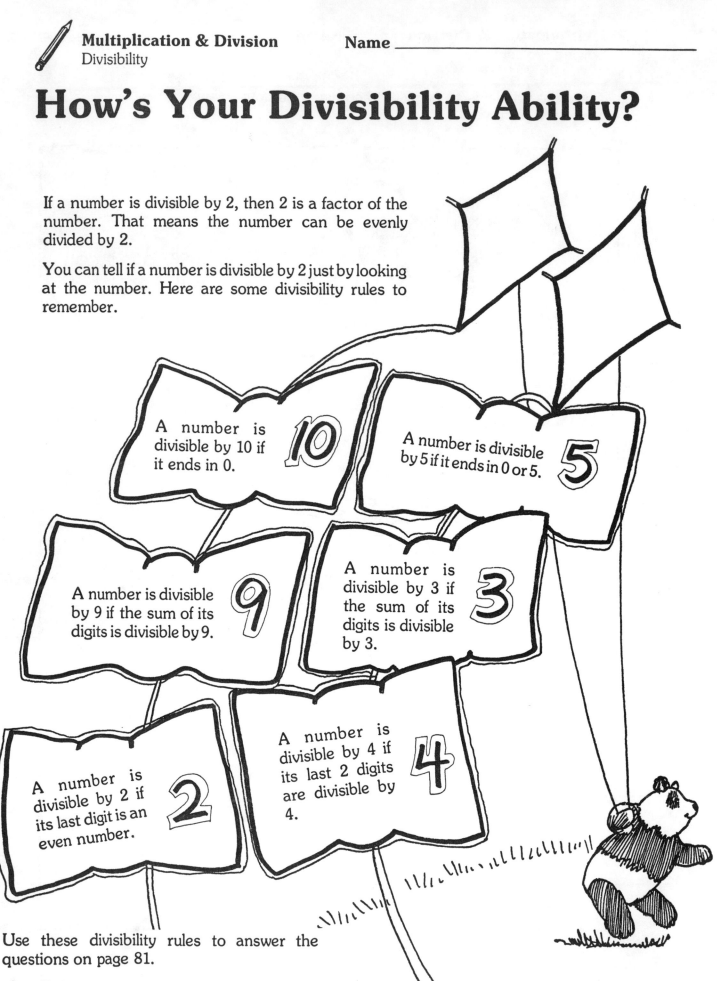

A number is divisible by 10 if it ends in 0. **10**

A number is divisible by 5 if it ends in 0 or 5. **5**

A number is divisible by 9 if the sum of its digits is divisible by 9. **9**

A number is divisible by 3 if the sum of its digits is divisible by 3. **3**

A number is divisible by 2 if its last digit is an even number. **2**

A number is divisible by 4 if its last 2 digits are divisible by 4. **4**

Use these divisibility rules to answer the questions on page 81.

Name _____

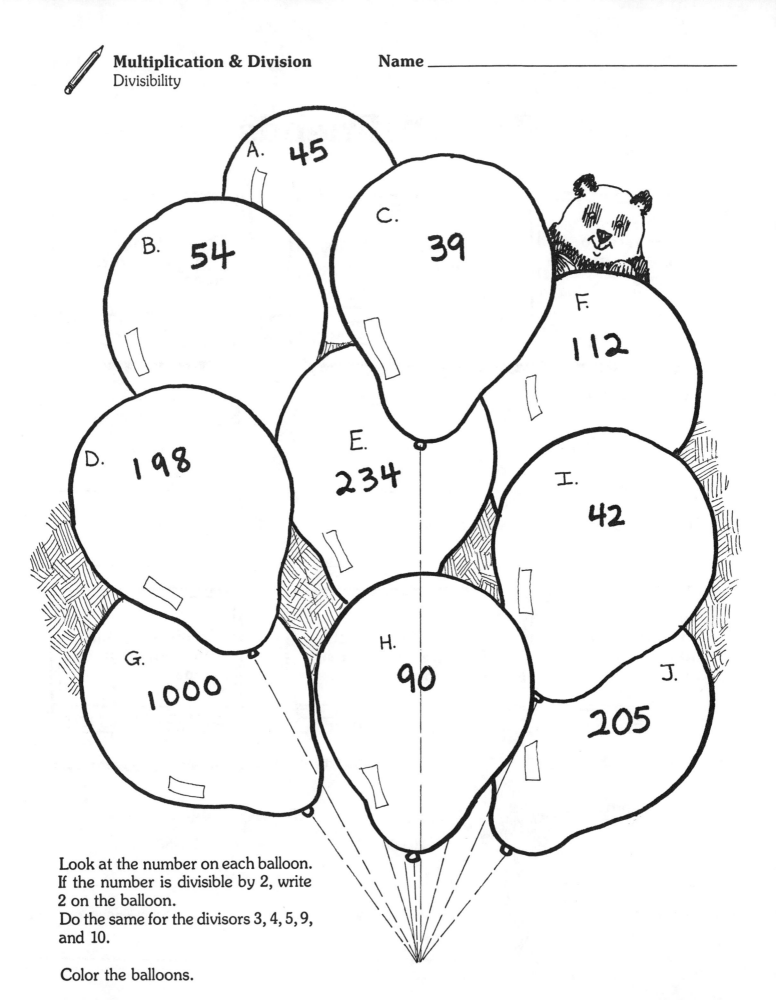

A. 45

B. 54

C. 39

F. 112

D. 198

E. 234

I. 42

G. 1000

H. 90

J. 205

Look at the number on each balloon. If the number is divisible by 2, write 2 on the balloon.

Do the same for the divisors 3, 4, 5, 9, and 10.

Color the balloons.

Answers on page 239.

81

Name _____

Tens & Friends

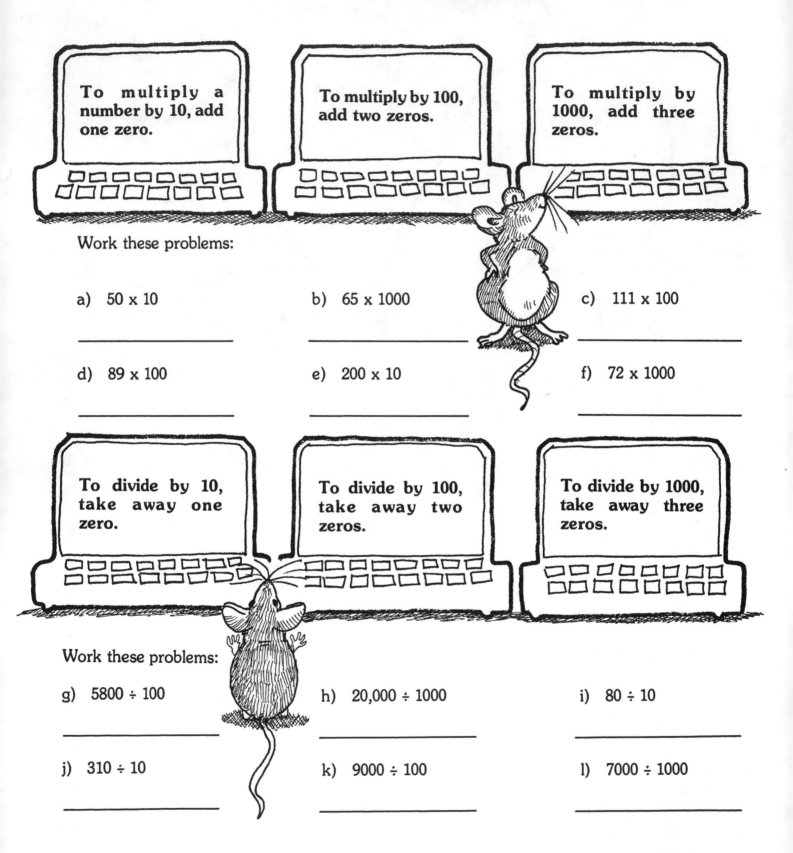

To multiply a number by 10, add one zero.

To multiply by 100, add two zeros.

To multiply by 1000, add three zeros.

Work these problems:

a) 50 x 10

_____

b) 65 x 1000

_____

c) 111 x 100

_____

d) 89 x 100

_____

e) 200 x 10

_____

f) 72 x 1000

_____

To divide by 10, take away one zero.

To divide by 100, take away two zeros.

To divide by 1000, take away three zeros.

Work these problems:

g) 5800 ÷ 100

_____

h) 20,000 ÷ 1000

_____

i) 80 ÷ 10

_____

j) 310 ÷ 10

_____

k) 9000 ÷ 100

_____

l) 7000 ÷ 1000

_____

Fractions & Decimals

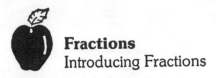
Domino Fractions

Preparation:

- Collect several sets of dominoes.

Use:

Dominoes are a great help for students just beginning to read, write, and understand fractions. After all, each domino is a fraction. Here are some ways you can use dominoes:

1) Draw a large domino on the board and help students see how it can be read as a fraction. Let the students identify the numerator and the denominator. Write the fraction on the board.
2) Give each student 10 or more dominoes. Ask the students to write fractions for the dominoes.
3) Have students work in pairs using dominoes as "flashcards" to practice reading fractions.
4) Students will enjoy this game. Call out a fractional number and ask the student who has the corresponding domino to shout "domino!"

$$= \frac{3}{6} \qquad = \frac{2}{4}$$

. . . And More Dominoes

Here are ways to use dominoes for learning and practicing more difficult fraction concepts.

1) Give each student two dominoes. Have the students look at the two fractions, find the least common multiple for the two denominators, and write the fractions with like denominators.
2) Use dominoes to create and solve addition and subtraction problems.
3) Give each student a group of dominoes and ask him or her to identify which fractions are in lowest terms. Ask the students to reduce those fractions that are not in lowest terms.
4) Give each student one domino and ask him or her to write three equivalent fractions.

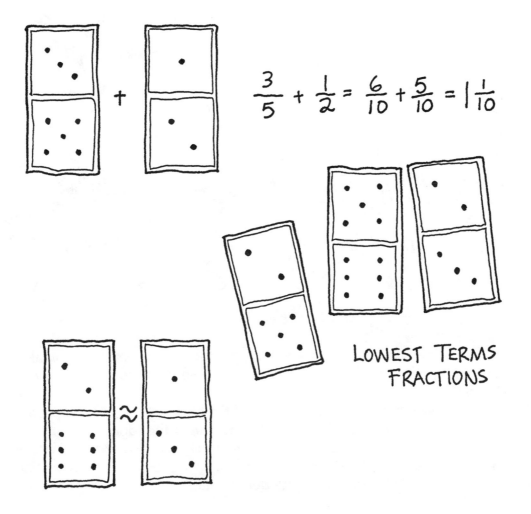

$$\frac{3}{5} + \frac{1}{2} = \frac{6}{10} + \frac{5}{10} = 1\frac{1}{10}$$

LOWEST TERMS
FRACTIONS

Teacher Page

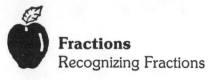
Fractions Good Enough To Eat

Preparation:
- Bring foods that can be cut into fractions to class (cucumbers, carrots, celery sticks, pretzels, graham crackers, fig newtons, small sandwiches, rice cakes, bananas, olives, etc.).

Use:
1) Have a fraction picnic. Sit on a rug in the classroom, on a blanket outdoors, or at a table in the cafeteria and "sample" fractions of various foods.
2) Cut or break the food items in front of the students, saying the proper fraction for the part of the whole before eating the food.
3) This activity may be used to concretely demonstrate the concept of mixed numerals. (It is also a good way to show the addition and subtraction of fractions with like denominators.)

 **Fractions**
Writing Fractions

Name _____

You're Being Watched!

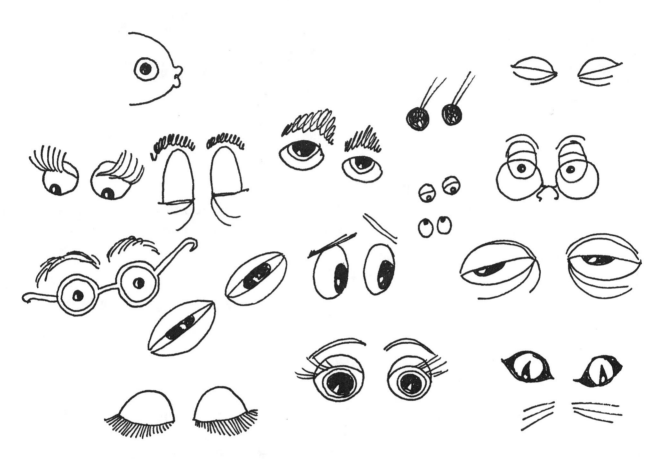

Answer each question below by writing a fraction (the numerator answers the question and the denominator tells how many eyes there are in all).

1) How many eyes are open? _____ closed? _____

2) How many eyes have eyelids? _____ bushy eyebrows? _____

3) How many eyes have no eyebrows? _____ wear glasses? _____

4) How many eyes are completely closed? _____ have lashes? _____

Answers on page 239.

Student Page

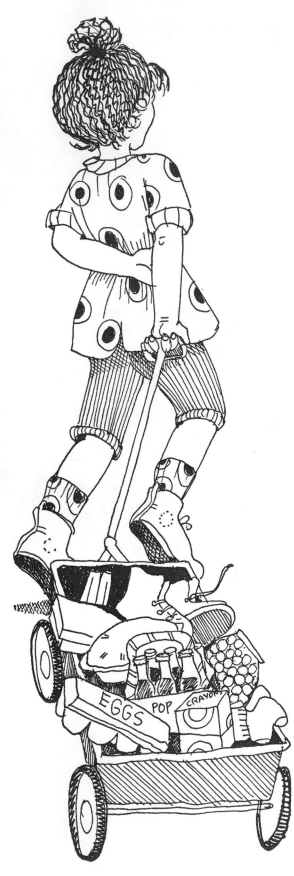

All Around The Town

Preparation:

- Bring into the classroom everyday objects that represent fractions. For example:

box of 8 crayons	one dozen eggs
six-pack of soda pop	pound of butter (sticks)
muffin tin	two-stick Popsicle
a pie cut into pieces	bag of marbles
pair of shoes	box of chocolates

Use:

1) Use the objects that are sets (ie: group of marbles, jacks, shoes, eggs) to help students see that a fraction is used to describe a part of a set.

2) Use the whole objects (ie: pie, butter, loaf of bread, etc.) to show that a fraction can also tell about parts of a whole.

3) Let the students search for sets and objects that can be used for illustrating fractions. Give the students time to ask one another questions which must be answered with fractions.

4) Follow this activity with the student page "Popsicles, Pizza & Pies" (page 89).

Name _____

Popsicles, Pizza & Pies

Write a fraction to answer each question below.

1). How much of the Popsicle is left?

2). How much of the pizza was eaten?

3). How much of the doughnut is left?

4). How much of the chocolate bar has been eaten?

5). How much of the pie is left?

6). How much of the soda is gone?

Draw a line from each picture to the fraction that shows what is left.

$\frac{1}{2}$

$\frac{5}{6}$

$\frac{2}{3}$

$\frac{7}{8}$

$\frac{2}{5}$

89

Fold-It-Yourself Fractions

Preparation:
- Cut 11 circles of the same size for each student out of sturdy white paper (a 20 cm circle is a good size).
- The students will need scissors, glue, and crayons.

Use:
1) Pages 91-93 give directions for folding and cutting circles into fractional parts. These circles can be used for many of the fraction concepts you'll be teaching. For example:

   - Introducing fractions of various sizes
   - Comparing fraction sizes
   - Reading and writing fractions
   - Finding equivalent fractions
   - Addition and subtraction with like denominators

2) Each student should have a set of circles at his or her desk in order to follow along with group activities or to solve problems individually. Encourage the students to color and add designs to their fraction sets.
3) Sections of circles may be cut and pasted onto another sheet of paper for some activities.

Fractions
Recognizing Fractions

Name _____

1. **Whole**

Leave the circle just as it is.

2. **Halves**

Fold the circle in half. Cut along the crease to make two equal pieces.

3. **Thirds**

Fold the circle in half. Now fold $\frac{1}{3}$ of the half toward the middle. Then fold over the remaining third. Open the circle. You will see six equal parts. Cut on every other crease to make thirds.

4. **Fourths**

Fold the circle in half. Then fold the circle in half again. Cut along every crease to make four equal parts.

Student Page

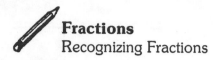

5. Fifths

Fold the circle in half. Fold $\frac{1}{5}$ of the half toward the center. Fold that fifth toward the center three more times. Open the circle. You will see ten equal parts. Cut on every other crease to make fifths.

6. Sixths

Fold the circle in half. Fold $\frac{1}{3}$ of the half toward the middle. Then fold over the remaining third. Open the circle. You will see six equal parts. Cut on every crease to make sixths.

7. Sevenths

Fold the circle in half. Then fold $\frac{1}{7}$ of the half toward the center. Continue folding the seventh toward the center five more times. Open the circle. You will see 14 equal parts. Cut on every other crease to make sevenths.

8. Eighths

Fold the circle in half. Fold the circle in half two more times. Open the circle. You will see eight equal parts. Cut along each crease to make eigths.

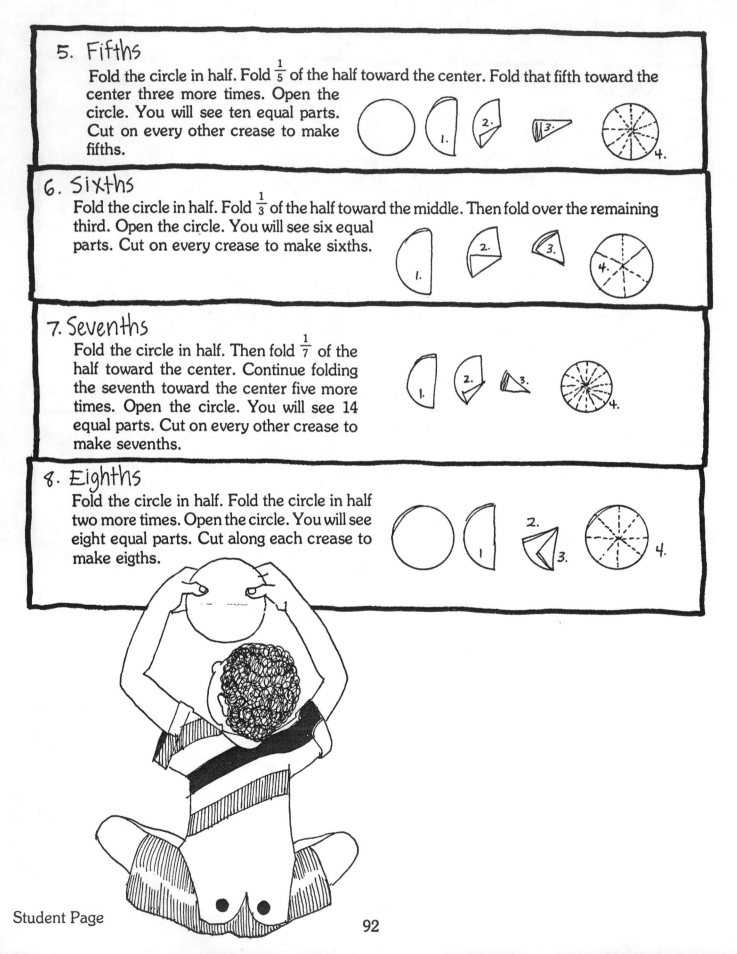

9. Ninths

Fold the circle in half. Then fold $\frac{1}{3}$ of the half toward the center. Fold over the remaining third to make three sections out of the half. Now fold $\frac{1}{3}$ of this piece toward the center. Fold the remaining third toward the center. Open the circle. You will see 18 equal parts. Cut along every other crease to make ninths.

10. Tenths

Fold the circle in half. Fold $\frac{1}{5}$ of the half toward the center. Fold that fifth toward the center three more times. Open the circle. You will see ten equal parts. Cut along every crease to make tenths.

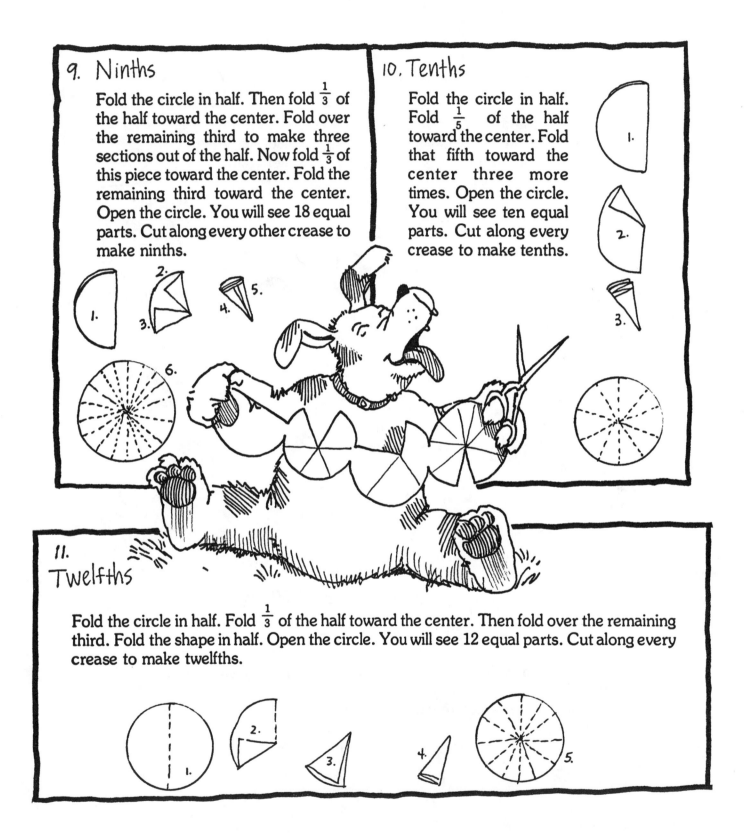

11. Twelfths

Fold the circle in half. Fold $\frac{1}{3}$ of the half toward the center. Then fold over the remaining third. Fold the shape in half. Open the circle. You will see 12 equal parts. Cut along every crease to make twelfths.

Student Page

Factor Factory

This machine inspects fractions to find out if they are in lowest terms.

It finds the factors of the numerator.

And it finds the factors of the denominator.

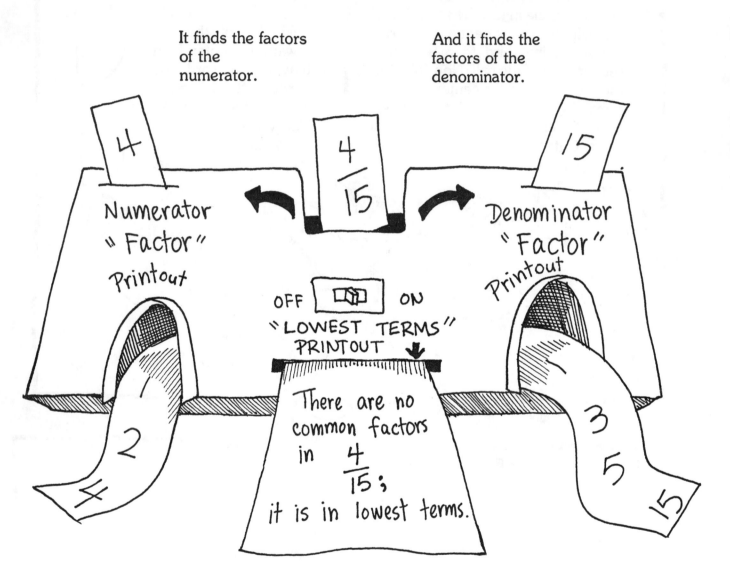

If none of the factors are the same, then the fraction is in lowest terms.

(Factors that are the same are called common factors.)

Go to work in this factor factory. Write the factors for each fraction and then tell if the fraction is in lowest terms.

$$\frac{2}{4} \qquad \frac{6}{7} \qquad \frac{8}{12} \qquad \frac{9}{10}$$

This machine reduces fractions to lowest terms.

First, it gives the factors.

Numerator:

1, 3, 9

Denominator:

1, 15, 3, 5

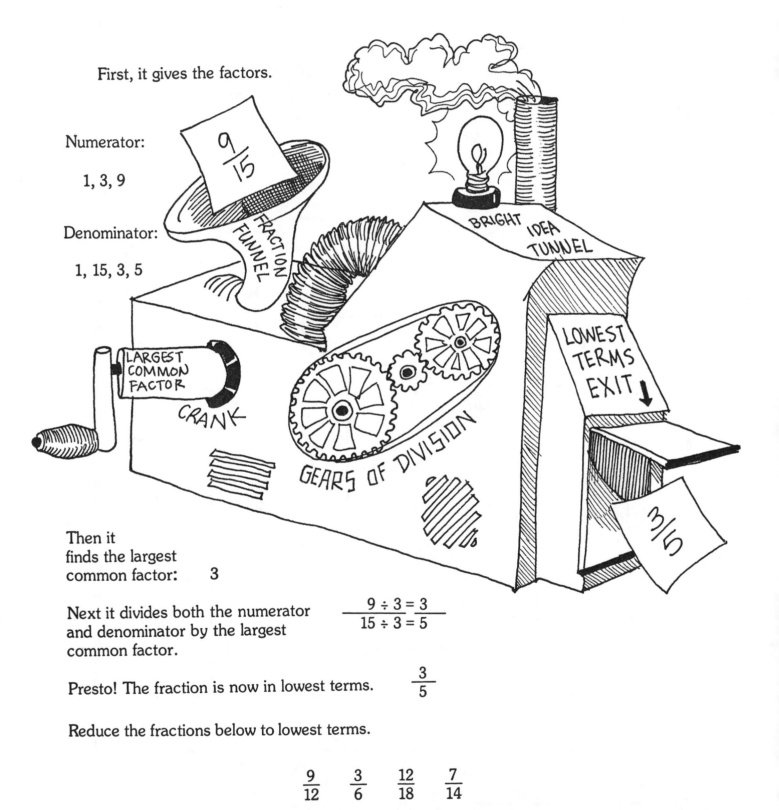

Then it
finds the largest
common factor: 3

Next it divides both the numerator
and denominator by the largest
common factor.

$$\frac{9 \div 3 = 3}{15 \div 3 = 5}$$

Presto! The fraction is now in lowest terms. $\frac{3}{5}$

Reduce the fractions below to lowest terms.

$$\frac{9}{12} \qquad \frac{3}{6} \qquad \frac{12}{18} \qquad \frac{7}{14}$$

Name _____

A-maze-ing Fractions

You must help Rufus Rat get to the cheese.

Begin at "start" and draw a line through the maze following fractions that are in lowest terms.

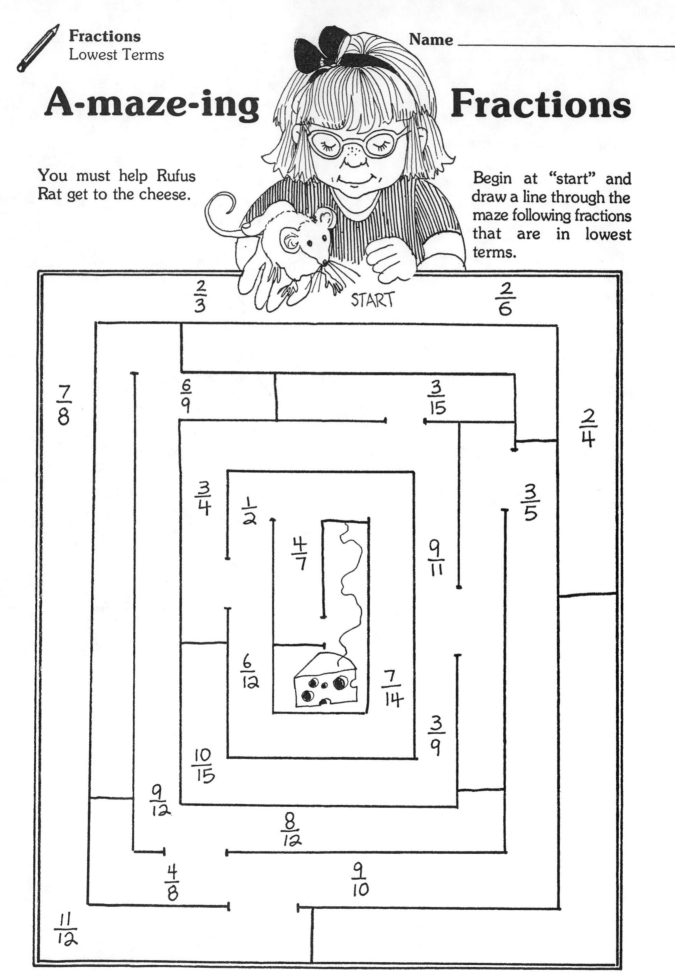

START

$\frac{2}{3}$ $\frac{2}{6}$

$\frac{7}{8}$ $\frac{6}{9}$ $\frac{3}{15}$ $\frac{2}{4}$

$\frac{3}{4}$ $\frac{1}{2}$ $\frac{3}{5}$

$\frac{4}{7}$ $\frac{9}{11}$

$\frac{6}{12}$ $\frac{7}{14}$

$\frac{3}{9}$

$\frac{10}{15}$

$\frac{9}{12}$

$\frac{8}{12}$

$\frac{4}{8}$ $\frac{9}{10}$

$\frac{11}{12}$

Name _____

Would You Rather?

Ask each question below to ten classmates. Write a fraction to show how many of your classmates chose each answer. Be sure to write the fraction in lowest terms.

1. Would you rather swallow a frog or eat worm soup?

2. Would you rather ride on a witch's broom or learn to cast magic spells?

3. Would you rather find a crocodile in your bed or have lunch with a lobster?

4. Would you rather go for a swim in broccoli soup or sleep in mashed potatoes?

5. Would you rather turn into a tiny elf or a huge giant?

6. Would you rather live in an igloo or move into a houseboat on the ocean?

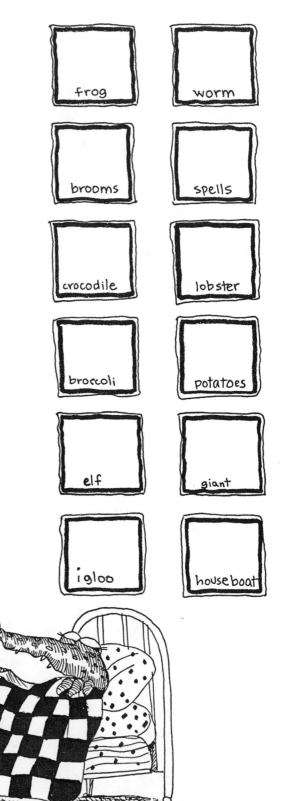

frog   worm

brooms   spells

crocodile   lobster

broccoli   potatoes

elf   giant

igloo   houseboat

97

Student Page

Eggs-Citement

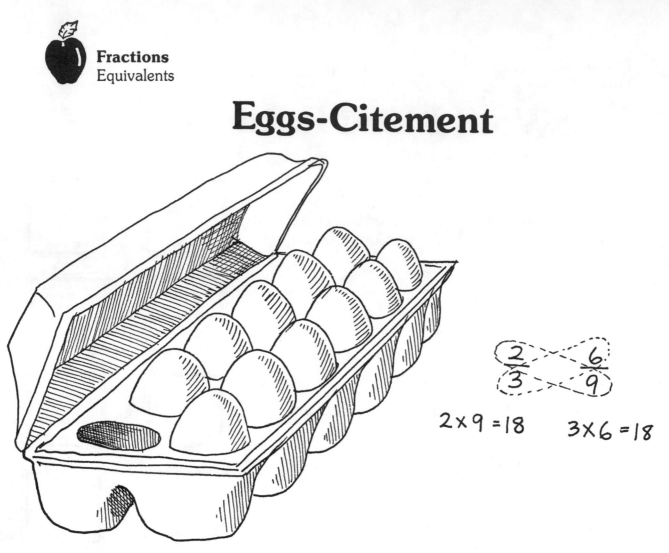

$$\frac{2}{3} \quad \frac{6}{9}$$

$$2 \times 9 = 18 \qquad 3 \times 6 = 18$$

Uh oh!

Preparation:
- You will need copies of the student page "Equal Treatment" (page 99) and a dozen eggs in an egg carton.

Use:

1) Use the eggs to demonstrate the concept of equivalent fractions. Show the students how $\frac{1}{2}$, $\frac{2}{4}$, $\frac{6}{12}$, and $\frac{3}{6}$ represent the same amount. Then show that $\frac{1}{3}$, $\frac{2}{6}$, and $\frac{4}{12}$ represent the same amount.

2) Teach the students how to tell if two fractions are equivalent. Let the students practice determining equivalents with several pairs of fractions.

   Cross-multiply.

   If the two products are the same, then the fractions are equivalent.

3) Hand out copies of the student page and help the students learn how to find and write equivalent fractions.

Name _____

Equal Treatment

Think of a fraction as a pair of kids in a bunk bed who want to be treated equally.

Whatever one gets, the other one wants!

If you multiply the numerator and denominator by the same thing, you will get an equivalent fraction.

$\frac{4}{6}$ is equivalent to $\frac{2}{3}$.

You can write it like this:

$$\frac{2}{3} = \frac{4}{6}$$

Try it again. This time multiply by 3.

The equivalent fraction is _____ .

Write an equivalent fraction for each of the fractions below.

$\frac{1}{2}$ ☐ $\frac{3}{4}$ ☐ $\frac{4}{5}$ ☐

Student Page

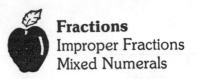

Where Have All The Caterpillars Gone?

Preparation:

- Make large green or brown caterpillars using construction paper. (You may wish to have students make these.) Write an improper fraction on each caterpillar.
- Have on hand bright colors of construction paper, black construction paper, scissors, glue, markers, and crayons. Also, gather books that have pictures of butterflies and moths.

Use:

1) After explaining improper fractions to the class and demonstrating how to change improper fractions into mixed numerals, show the students a construction paper caterpillar. Ask the class to write the mixed numeral that equals the improper fraction written on the caterpillar.

2) Give each student a caterpillar. Instruct each student to make a butterfly using the provided materials and to write the improper fraction as a mixed numeral on the butterfly.

3) Let the students match the butterflies and caterpillars on the student page "Something Has Changed!" (page 101).

Name _____

Something Has Changed!

A. From which caterpillar did each butterfly come? Draw a line to match the improper fractions and the mixed numerals.

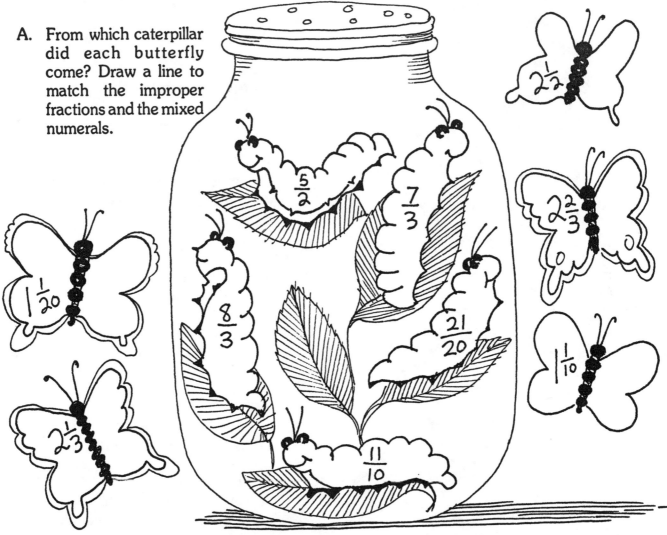

B. What will the improper fractions on these caterpillars become when the caterpillars change into butterflies? Draw a butterfly beside each caterpillar. Write the correct mixed numeral on each butterfly.

Witch One?

Preparation:
- Make a large witch to display on a bulletin board. (Students may help draw and paint the witch.) Label the display "Witch One?"
- Write mixed numerals (one digit for the whole number) on index cards.
- Have drawing paper and crayons available.

Use:

After reviewing mixed numerals with the class, reinforce the concept with the witch display.

1) Explain the play on words in the title of the bulletin board. Practice spelling "witch" and "which" and help the students discriminate between the two.

2) Give each student an index card (with a mixed numeral) and a piece of drawing paper. Direct the students to draw something that a witch might use which shows the mixed numeral. For example:

   $2\frac{1}{2}$ bottles of magic potion
   $6\frac{3}{4}$ bat-wing pies

3) Display the pictures with the witch. Place the index cards in a pocket attached to the board.

4) Students may enjoy working individually or in pairs to choose a card from the board and find the matching picture.

Dig For Treasure

What treasure pictured here is in each chest below? Find the answer for each problem and write it on the treasure. Then draw a line to match each treasure to the correct chest.

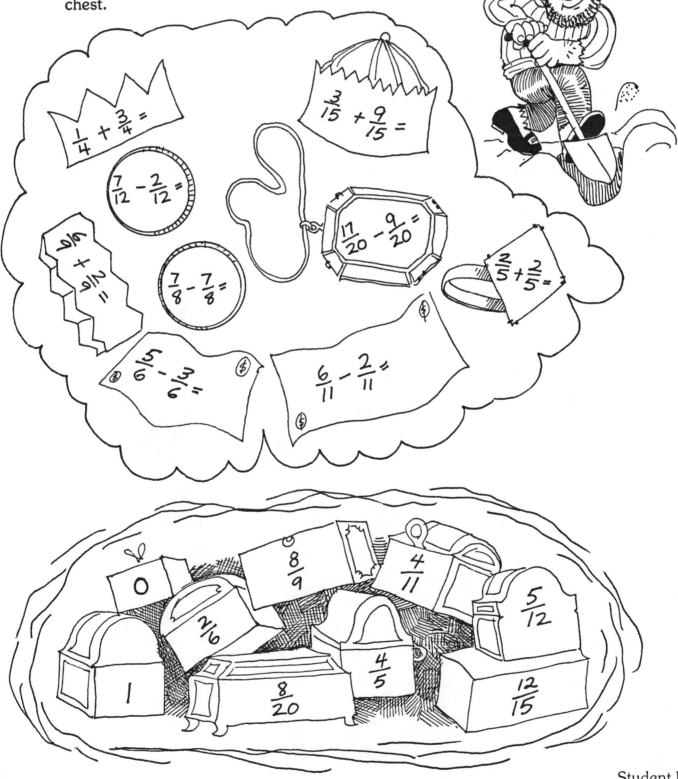

$\frac{1}{4} + \frac{3}{4} =$

$\frac{3}{15} + \frac{9}{15} =$

$\frac{7}{12} - \frac{2}{12} =$

$\frac{6}{9} + \frac{2}{9} =$

$\frac{17}{20} - \frac{9}{20} =$

$\frac{7}{8} - \frac{7}{8} =$

$\frac{2}{5} + \frac{2}{5} =$

$\frac{5}{6} - \frac{3}{6} =$

$\frac{6}{11} - \frac{2}{11} =$

0

$\frac{8}{9}$

$\frac{4}{11}$

$\frac{2}{6}$

$\frac{5}{12}$

1

$\frac{8}{20}$

$\frac{4}{5}$

$\frac{12}{15}$

Student Page

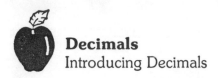

Decimal Squares

Preparation:
- You will need lots of graph paper (with squares of at least 1 cm), crayons and scissors.

Use:
1) Have each student cut ten squares from graph paper, each 10 x 10. Each 10 x 10 square has 100 small squares, allowing you to discuss decimal numerals having tenths and hundredths.
2) The squares will help students visualize decimal numerals. For example, students can visualize 2.3 by coloring two 10 x 10 squares and three rows of ten individual squares on another 10 x 10 square.

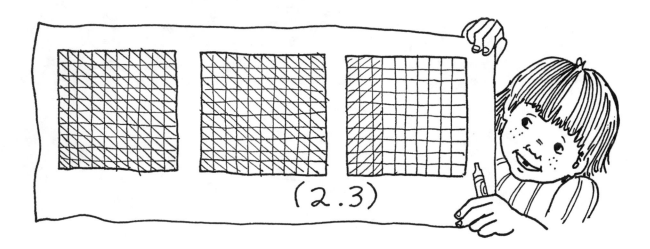

(2.3)

3) Work with the students to illustrate other decimals such as:

1.8	2.15	0.13
3.77	0.06	4.9

Name _____

Crazy About Squares

Molly McMouse has "gone crazy" coloring squares!
Write a decimal for each numbered picture below to show how much Molly has colored.

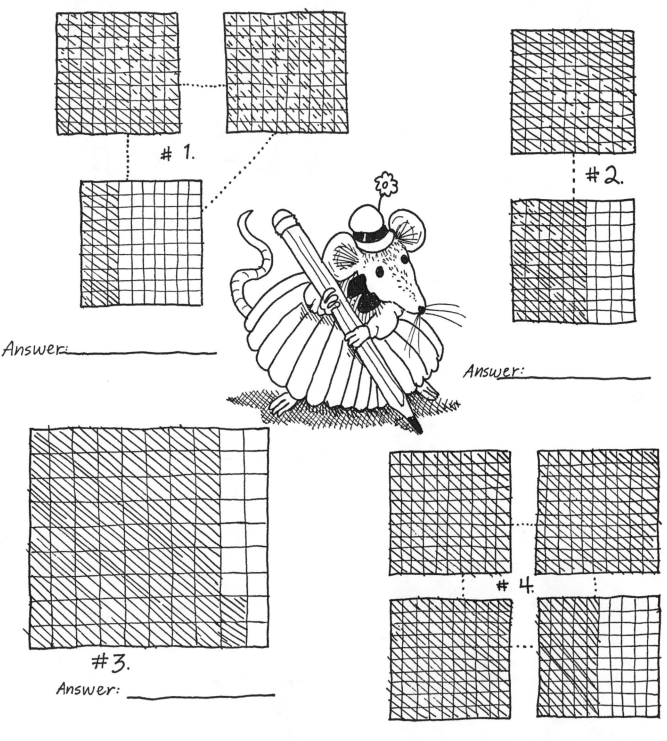

1.

2.

Answer: _____

Answer: _____

#3.

Answer: _____

4.

Answer: _____

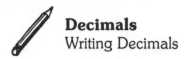

Decimals
Writing Decimals

Name _____

Follow That Centipede

Hello! I am Cynthia Centipede. Help me
learn about decimals by answering
each question below with
a decimal. The first
one is done for
you.

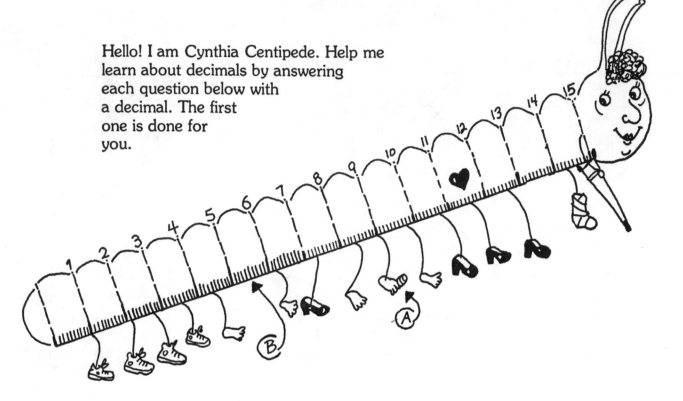

1) I fell and broke one leg. Where is that leg? _____ 14.3 _____

2) Which feet are not wearing shoes? ____ , ____ , ____ , ____ , ____ , ____

3) Where is my ingrown toenail (A)? _____

4) Arrow B points to my tummy ache. Where is it? _____

5) Which feet are wearing high heels? ____ , ____ , ____ , ____

6) Which feet are wearing jogging shoes? ____ , ____ , ____ , ____

7) Where is my heart? _____

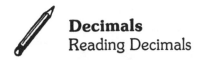

Name _____

What? Another Centipede?

I'm Cynthia's friend, Charlie. Follow the instructions below to make me complete.

1) Draw a heart at about 2.3.

2) Draw blue shoes at 6.5 and 12.2.

3) Draw a tie at 0.2.

4) Draw a ribbon at 15.0.

5) Color red stripes at 7.0, 3.1, and 14.2.

6) Color green stripes at 2.1 and 9.6.

7) I have a cut on my foot at 10.5. Please put a bandage on it.

Student Page

Name _____

Decimals  Everywhere

Remember:
When you add or subtract decimals, you must line up numbers by the decimal point.

ADD:

A)   3.5 inches of snow
          12.8 inches of snow
          0.4 inch of snow
    +   1.1 inches of snow
          _____ inches of snow

B)   50.35 miles
           9.6 miles
    +   0.77 miles
          _____ miles

SUBTRACT:

D)   55.235 tons
    -      4.11 tons
          _____ tons

C)   1999.99 cupcakes
    -      333.03 cupcakes
          _____ cupcakes

E)   485.3 chocolate bars
    -      42.0 chocolate bars
          _____ chocolate bars

F)   88.80 years
    -      4.50 years
          _____ years

108

Answers on page 239.

Decimals
Adding & Subtracting

Name _____

Write each problem and then solve it.

G) Monday we drove 225.7 km. Tuesday we drove 100.55 km. How long was the trip?

H) I weigh 75.8 pounds. My baby sister weighs 20.8 pounds. What is the difference in our weights?

I) Jamie's temperature is 2.9° above normal. Normal body temperature is 37.0° C. What is Jamie's temperature?

J) Bill can run 4.7 miles per hour. His lizard can run 8.3 miles per hour. How much faster is the lizard?

K) The wind blew 22.7 km per hour yesterday. Today the wind is blowing 15.5 km per hour faster. What's the wind speed today?

Name _____

About How Much?

Circle the decimal that is the most accurate answer.

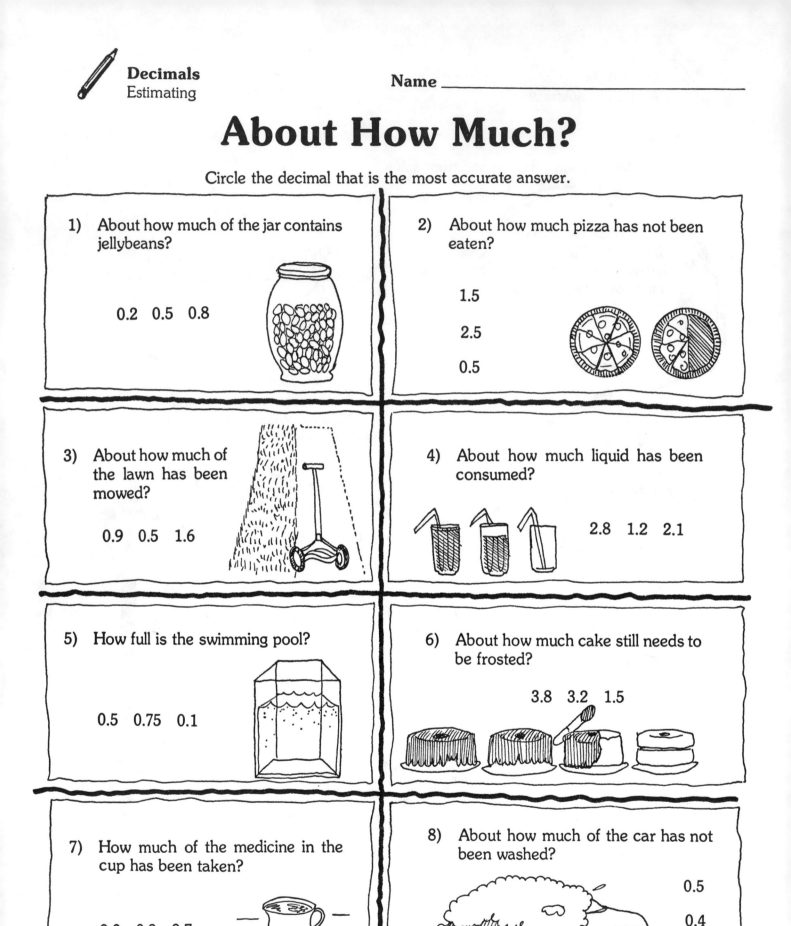

1) About how much of the jar contains jellybeans?

0.2   0.5   0.8

2) About how much pizza has not been eaten?

1.5

2.5

0.5

3) About how much of the lawn has been mowed?

0.9   0.5   1.6

4) About how much liquid has been consumed?

2.8   1.2   2.1

5) How full is the swimming pool?

0.5   0.75   0.1

6) About how much cake still needs to be frosted?

3.8   3.2   1.5

7) How much of the medicine in the cup has been taken?

0.0   0.3   0.7

8) About how much of the car has not been washed?

0.5

0.4

1.7

110

Answers on page 239.

Straw Geometry

Preparation:
- Make copies of the student pages "My Book Of Straw Geometry" (pages 113-114) for your students.
- Each student will need scissors and four plastic straws.

Use:

A straw is a fine example of a line segment and therefore an excellent tool for teaching geometric shapes and concepts. Here's how to explain lines and angles to young mathematicians.

1) Give each student four straws. Explain what a line is, and hold up a straw as an example of a line segment.

2) Ask the students to show you a line segment. They can actually hold up a straw so that it can be easily seen.

3) Continue to explain: intersecting line segments
                          parallel line segments
                          perpendicular line segments
                          angles
                          right angles
                          acute and obtuse angles
                          straight angles

Students can make each figure with straws. (You may wish to use straws to show plane figures such as squares, triangles, rectangles, etc.)

4) Give each student copies of pages 113 and 114 and help them cut apart the pages to make their own book. Once the books are stapled together, direct the students to follow the directions and complete the books.

My Book Of Straw Geometry

name: _____

1.

Use a straw to show a line segment on your desk.

Draw a line segment here.

2.

Use straws to show two intersecting line segments on your desk.

Draw them here.

3.

Use straws to show two parallel line segments on your desk.

Draw them here.

4.

Use straws to show two perpendicular line segments on your desk.

Draw them here.

5.

Use straws to show a right angle on your desk.

Draw it here.

6.

Use straws to show an acute angle on your desk.

Draw it here.

7.

Use straws to show an obtuse angle on your desk.

Draw it here.

8.

The Friendly Circle

Radius - a line segment that joins the center of a circle with any point on its
   circumference.
Diameter - a straight line segment passing through the center of a circle and
   terminating at the outermost boundary (double the radius).
Use a ruler to find the radius and diameter of each circle on this page.

Checking Out Angles

OBTUSE ANGLE

OBTUSE ANGLE
- any angle *greater* than a right angle

RIGHT ANGLE -
makes a perfect corner (90°)

RIGHT ANGLE

ACUTE ANGLE
↓
ACUTE ANGLE -
any angle *less* than a right angle

1. R A O

2. R A O

3. R A O

4. R A O

5. R A O

6. R A O

7. R A O

8. R A O

Crunchy Bits

Decide if each picture in the box illustrates a right angle, an acute angle, or an obtuse angle. Circle R, A, or O.

Geometry
Angles

Name _____

Look at these polygons and tell how many angles each has.

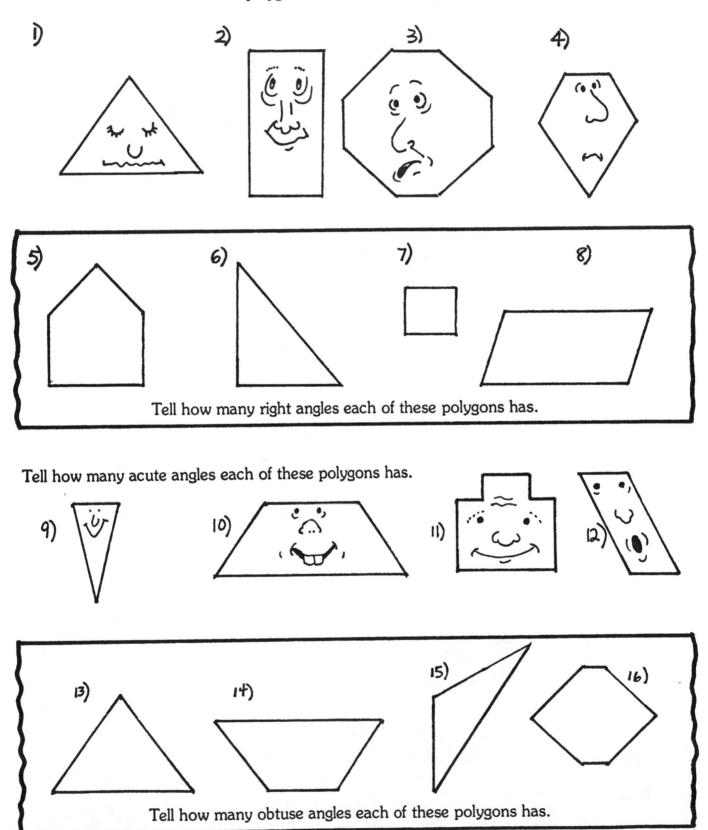

1)

2)

3)

4)

5) 6) 7) 8)

Tell how many right angles each of these polygons has.

Tell how many acute angles each of these polygons has.

9) 10) 11) 12)

13) 14) 15) 16)

Tell how many obtuse angles each of these polygons has.

Name _____

You're Surrounded By Polygons

How many polygons can you find in this picture?
Circle each polygon with a red crayon.

The Geo-chart on page 119 will help you.

See if you can find at least one of each kind!

Name _____

Geo-Chart

Polygon   Illustration   Description

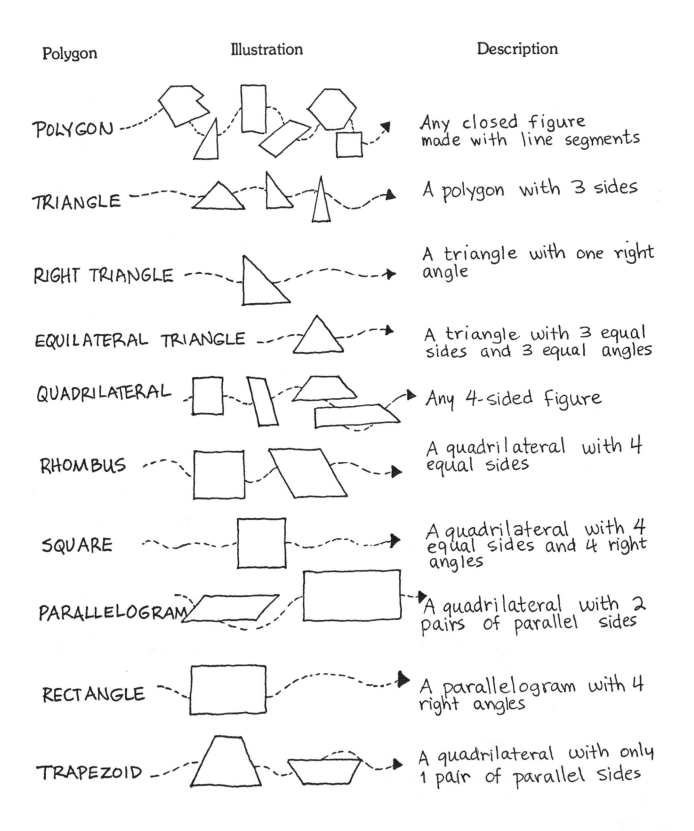

POLYGON — Any closed figure made with line segments

TRIANGLE — A polygon with 3 sides

RIGHT TRIANGLE — A triangle with one right angle

EQUILATERAL TRIANGLE — A triangle with 3 equal sides and 3 equal angles

QUADRILATERAL — Any 4-sided figure

RHOMBUS — A quadrilateral with 4 equal sides

SQUARE — A quadrilateral with 4 equal sides and 4 right angles

PARALLELOGRAM — A quadrilateral with 2 pairs of parallel sides

RECTANGLE — A parallelogram with 4 right angles

TRAPEZOID — A quadrilateral with only 1 pair of parallel sides

Student Page

Geo-Mat

Preparation:

- Use a permanent marker to draw plane figures on an old window shade or piece of vinyl to make a large geo-mat (see illustration).
- Be sure to include the following:

line	right angle	rectangle
curve	acute angle	circle
obtuse angle	right triangle	isosceles triangle
scalene triangle	square	quadrilateral
parallelogram	equilateral triangle	parallel lines

Use:

1) The geo-mat can be placed on the floor for teaching and reviewing plane figures. Gather a group of students around the mat and ask questions such as:

   Can you find a shape that has three sides? Put your hand on it. It's called a triangle.

2) Give directions such as:

   Put your hand on an acute angle.
   Put one foot on a quadrilateral.
   Put one hand on a circle and the other on a rectangle.

Ice Cream Cone Geometry

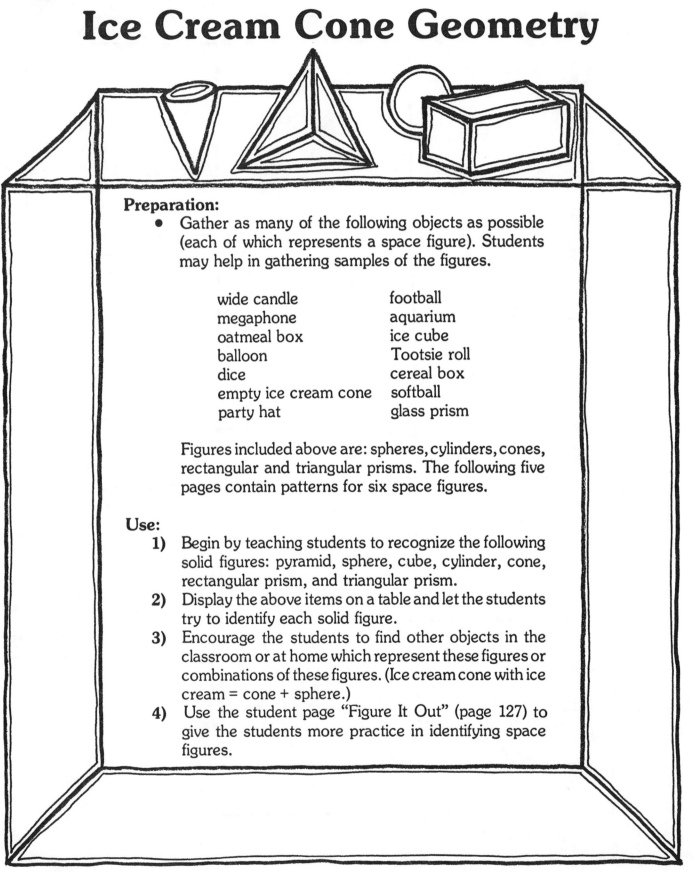

Preparation:
- Gather as many of the following objects as possible (each of which represents a space figure). Students may help in gathering samples of the figures.

wide candle	football
megaphone	aquarium
oatmeal box	ice cube
balloon	Tootsie roll
dice	cereal box
empty ice cream cone	softball
party hat	glass prism

Figures included above are: spheres, cylinders, cones, rectangular and triangular prisms. The following five pages contain patterns for six space figures.

Use:
1) Begin by teaching students to recognize the following solid figures: pyramid, sphere, cube, cylinder, cone, rectangular prism, and triangular prism.
2) Display the above items on a table and let the students try to identify each solid figure.
3) Encourage the students to find other objects in the classroom or at home which represent these figures or combinations of these figures. (Ice cream cone with ice cream = cone + sphere.)
4) Use the student page "Figure It Out" (page 127) to give the students more practice in identifying space figures.

Teacher Page

Cube
Pattern

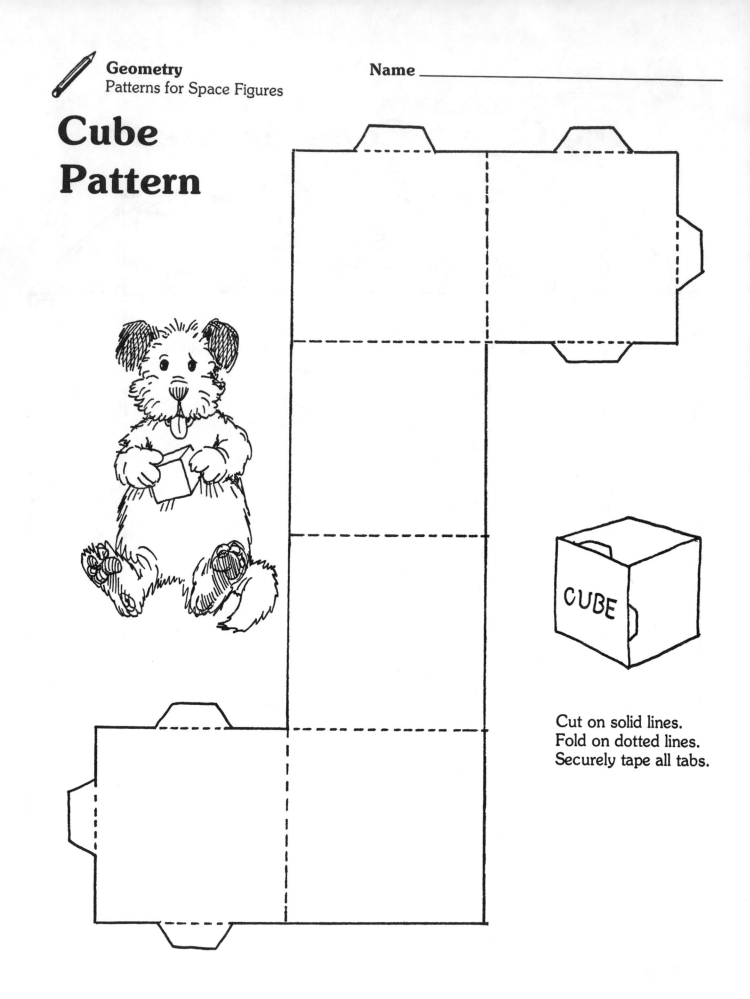

Cut on solid lines.
Fold on dotted lines.
Securely tape all tabs.

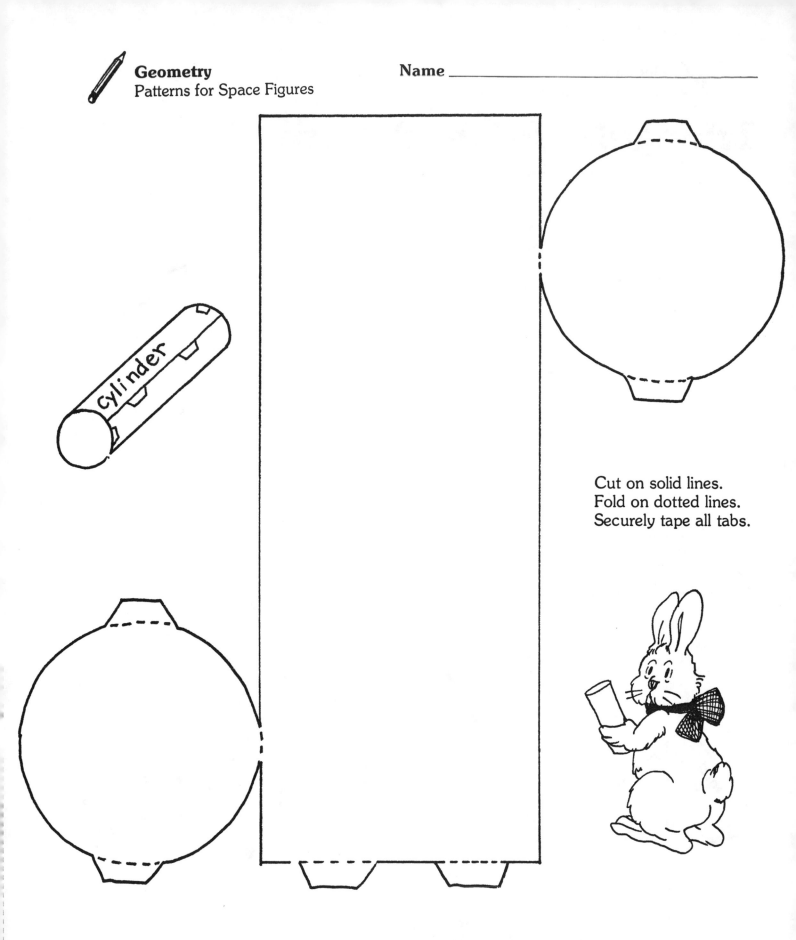

Cut on solid lines.
Fold on dotted lines.
Securely tape all tabs.

Cylinder Pattern

Student Page

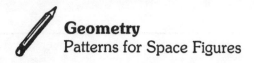

Triangular Prism Pattern

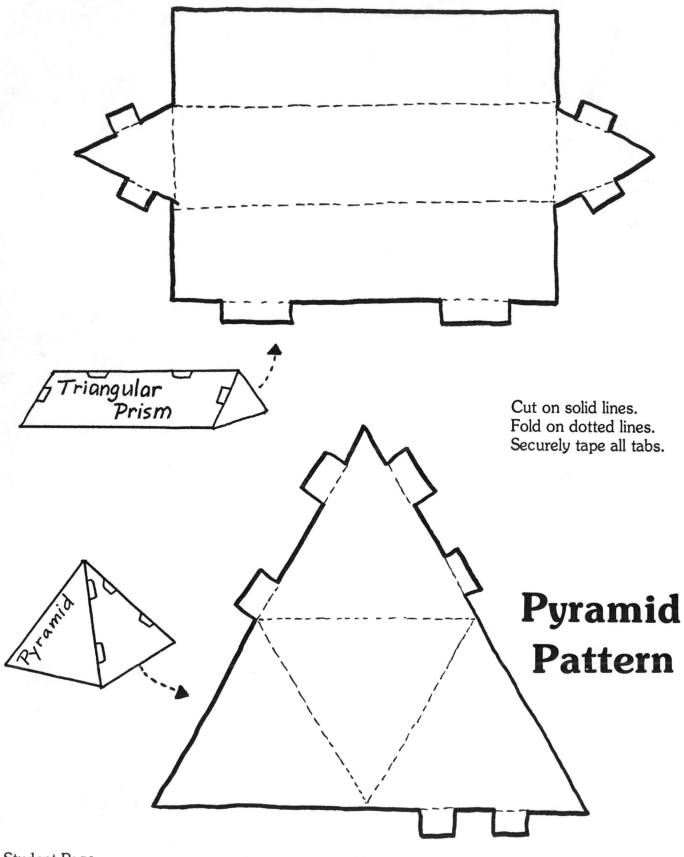

Cut on solid lines.
Fold on dotted lines.
Securely tape all tabs.

Pyramid Pattern

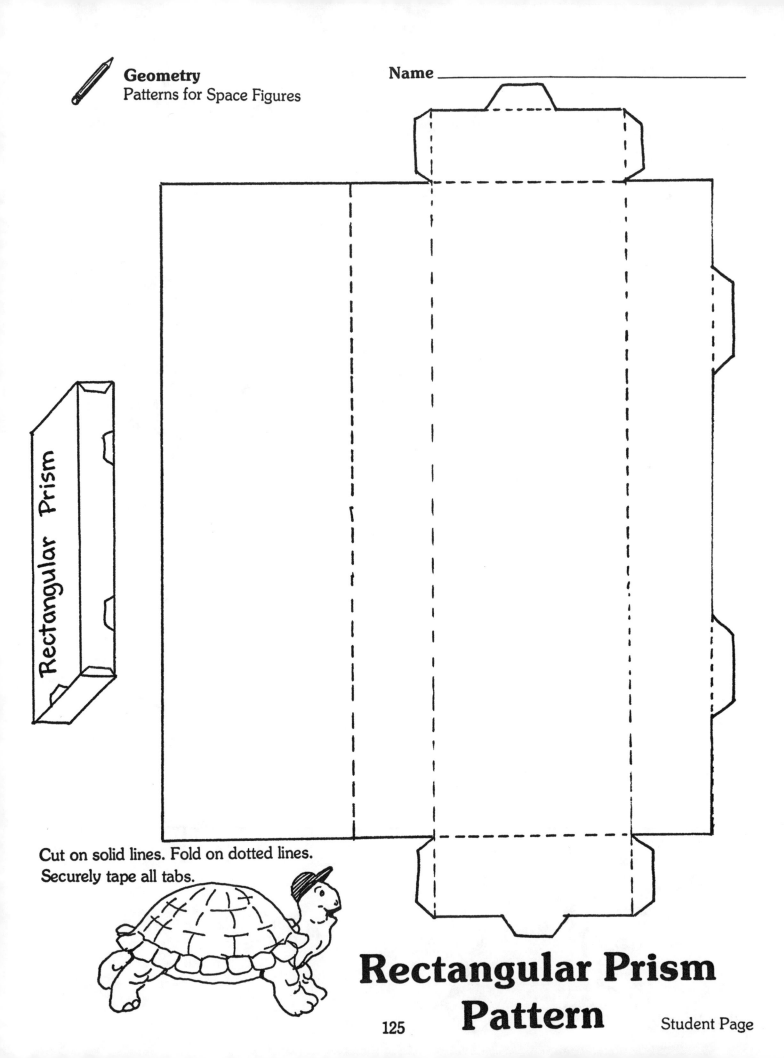

Name _____

Rectangular Prism

Cut on solid lines. Fold on dotted lines.
Securely tape all tabs.

Rectangular Prism
Pattern

125   Student Page

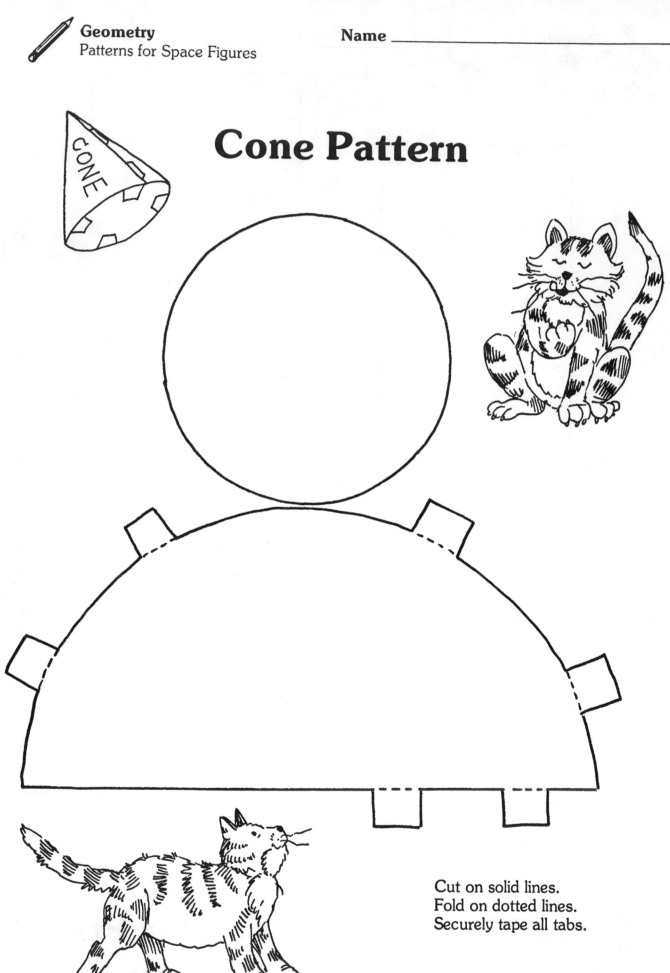

Cone Pattern

CONE

Cut on solid lines.
Fold on dotted lines.
Securely tape all tabs.

Name _____

Figure It Out

Find and circle these space figures in the picture below.

cylinder   cone   pyramid   sphere   triangular prism

Student Page

Paintings With Symmetry

Preparation:
- You'll need large white drawing paper, tempera paints and paintbrushes.

Use:

1) Explain the terms "line of symmetry" and "symmetric" to the students.

   A figure has a line of symmetry if it can be folded so that the two sides are exactly the same. If a figure can be folded in half so that two sides fit exactly on top of each other, it is called symmetric.

2) Have the students complete the student page "Unfinished Figures" (page 129) to increase their understanding of the concept of symmetry.

3) Let the students make symmetric paintings. Have the students fold drawing paper in half. The crease is to be the line of symmetry.

4) Next, have the students drop a blob or dribble of paint on one half of the paper. Then instruct them to fold the paper again and rub until the paint spreads in various directions.

5) Students may repeat the previous step adding two or more colors. Have students open their papers to reveal the finished symmetric designs and to let them dry. Ask the students to locate the line of symmetry.

Name _____

Unfinished Figures

Finish each picture to make it symmetric.

Are these pictures symmetric? Write yes or no by each one.

1. a cloud?

2. a flower?

a heart?

a rock?
3.

4. a ball?

5.

6.

8. the sun?

7. a leaf?

a hand?

Name _____

Look-Alikes

Two figures that have the same shape are similar to each other.

Two figures that have the same size and the same shape are congruent to each other.

Color the pictures.

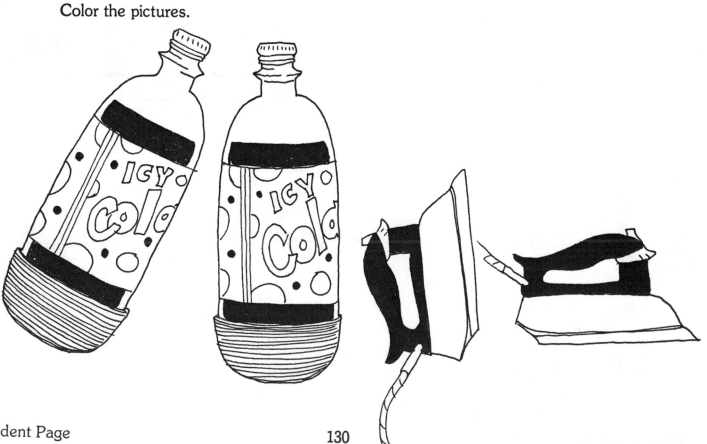

Name _____

How Good Are Your Eyes?

Find and circle the figure in each group that is similar to the first one.

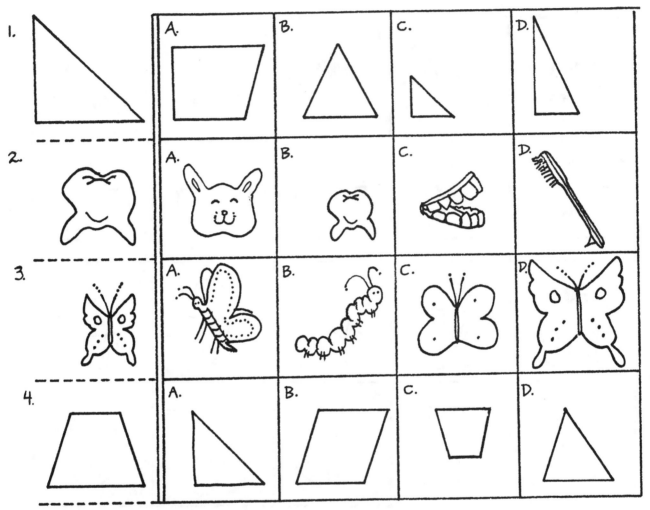

Draw a figure similar to each of these. Remember, it does not have to be the same size, but it does have to be the same shape.

Color the pictures.

Name _____

Just The Same

Find and circle the figure in each group that is congruent to the first one.

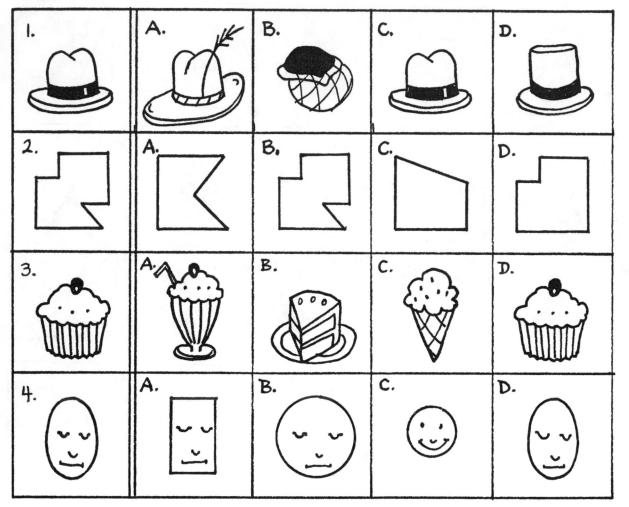

Draw a figure that is congruent to each of these.

Color the pictures.

How Many Pencils?

Preparation:
- Have several tools available for measuring — not the usual units, but units such as pencils, crayons, or paper clips.

Use:
1) Tell the students that they are going to be measuring their desks. Suggest that they use pencils to do it! Keep a record on the board of the measurements.
2) Measure desks with hands, fingers, or crayons. Again, compare measurements.
3) Have the students work in pairs to measure a desk with paper clips. Record the measurements.
4) Discuss the reasons for obtaining a variety of answers with measuring tools such as pencils, crayons, and hands. Ask students to consider and discuss the problems of measuring with objects that differ in length.
5) Help the students to see the need for a standard measurement unit. Name some of the common standard units. Have the students examine classroom measuring tools.

Name _____

Making Friends With A Centimeter

This is a centimeter. It is an important unit of measure. ⊢——⊣

Each of these objects measures approximately one centimeter.

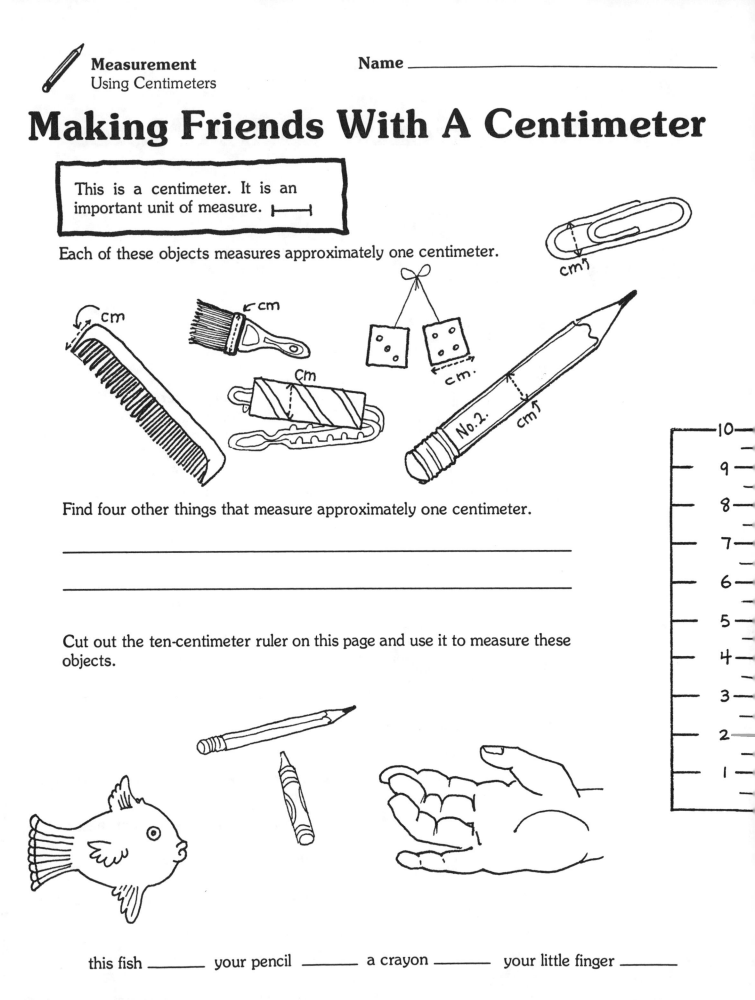

Find four other things that measure approximately one centimeter.

_____

_____

Cut out the ten-centimeter ruler on this page and use it to measure these objects.

this fish _____ your pencil _____ a crayon _____ your little finger _____

Student Page

Name _____

Making Friends With A Meter

A meter is 100 centimeters.
Ask your teacher for a meter stick.
Hold the meter stick next to you. Are you taller or shorter than one meter?
Measure the items below and write M, L, or E in the blank to show if the measurement is more than, less than, or equal to one meter.

_____ your friend's height

_____ your teacher's waist from the floor

_____ the distance between your hands (arms stretched out)

_____ the chalkboard height

How many meters are each of these?

the width of your classroom _____ m

the height of the classroom door _____ m

the distance from the floor
to the clock _____ m

Meters In Motion

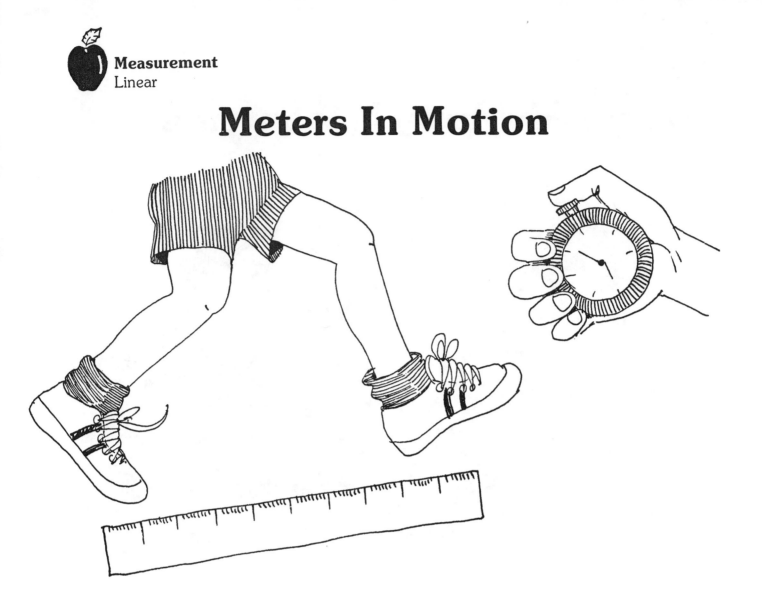

Preparation:
- This activity requires a day of good weather.
- You will need several meter sticks, a large piece of poster board (for a record chart), a marker and a stopwatch.

Use:

1) Take the class outdoors and line them up on two sides of a path or sidewalk.

2) Let the students take turns timing, measuring, and recording. Work together to find out:

How many meters can a student walk in 30 seconds?
How many meters can someone skip in 30 seconds?
How many meters can the teacher hop in 30 seconds?
How many meters can someone crawl in 30 seconds?
How many meters can someone run in 30 seconds?

Teacher Page

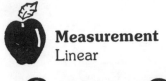

Some Shadowy Measurements

Preparation:
- You will need a sunny day, a group of students, measuring sticks, measuring tapes, and copies of the student page "Shadows Come In Several Sizes" (page 139).

Use:
1) Make sure that each student has a partner. Every pair of students will need a measuring stick or measuring tape, paper, and a copy of the student page.
2) Take the class outdoors. Demonstrate how your body can cast a shadow. Let two students measure your shadow so that all of the students can record the answer on their sheets.
3) Review the directions on the student page and let the students work in pairs to measure shadows of various objects and/or people.

Name _____

Shadows Come In Several Sizes

How long is each of these shadows?

Your teacher's   _____ cm

Your own   _____ cm

Your partner's   _____ cm

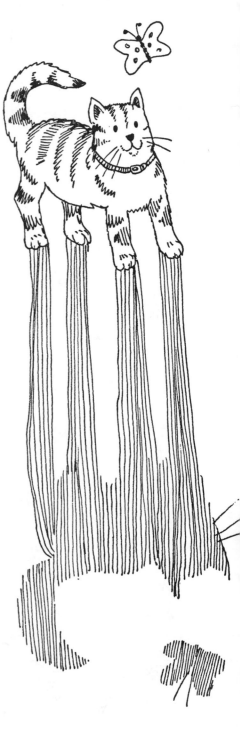

Find five other shadows to measure.

	Shadow Of →	Measurement →
shadow 1		
shadow 2		
shadow 3		
shadow 4		
shadow 5		

Fingers & Noses ... Tummies & Toes

Preparation:
- Collect metric measuring sticks.
- Cut several pieces of string, each to measure two meters.

Use:

1) Ask each student which he or she thinks is longer, the distance around his or her waist or the length of his or her arms? Discuss how you would measure waists, ankles, etc. when you have only measuring sticks. (Make lengths on string and then measure the string.)

2) Have the students make guesses about comparisons of other body measurements. Then have them measure to find out who's right.

3) Take time to let partners measure arms, noses, and wrists.

4) Give each student a copy of the student page "How I Measure Up" (page 141) and let students work in pairs to find the measurements. (Remind them to write their answers in centimeters.)

 **Measurement**
Linear

Name _____

Have a partner help you measure yourself to fill in the blanks below! Write your answers in centimeters.

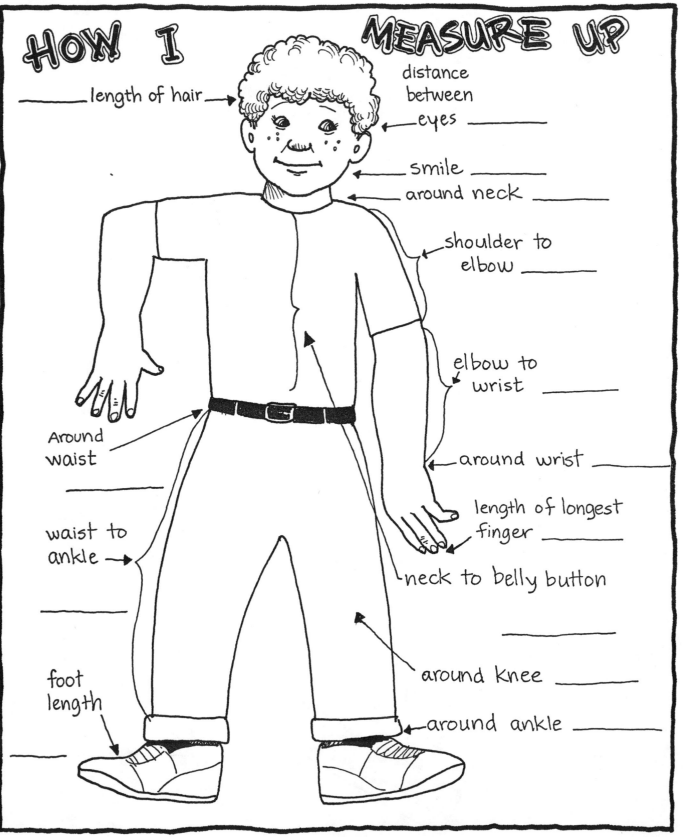

HOW I MEASURE UP

_____ length of hair →

distance between eyes _____

smile _____

around neck _____

shoulder to elbow _____

elbow to wrist _____

around wrist _____

length of longest finger _____

Around waist

_____

waist to ankle →

_____

foot length

neck to belly button

_____

around knee _____

around ankle _____

141

Name _____

All Around The Edge

Wally Worm crawls around the perimeter of things (the outer boundary).

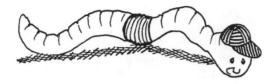

How far does Wally have to crawl to get around each of these objects?

Use a ruler to measure each side of the objects below. For every object, add the measurements together to find the perimeter of that object.

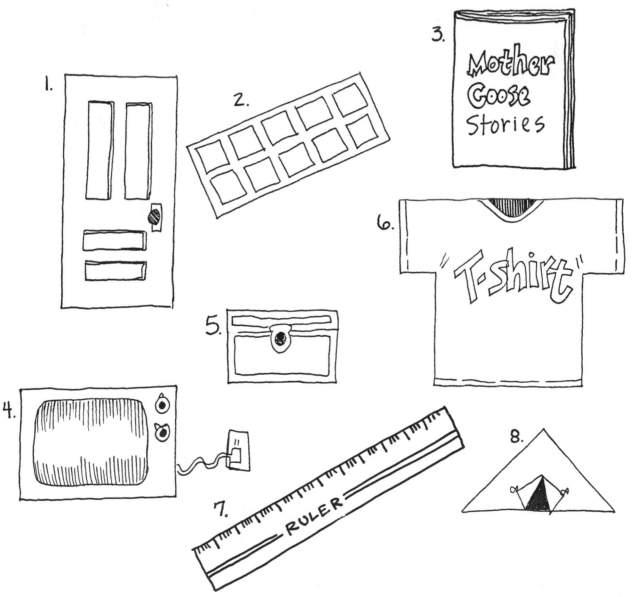

Name _____

Perimeters For Pythons

Today Wally Worm is visiting the zoo. He wants to crawl around the perimeters of animal cages. How far will he crawl around each of these?

1. MELVILLE MONKEY

2. MANDY PANDA

3. JERRY GIRAFFE

4. POLLY PYTHON

5. HENRY HIPPO

1 centimeter here equals
1 meter at the zoo.

Answers on page 240.

Student Page

Measurement
Area

The Great Cover-Up

Preparation:

- You will need a supply of centimeter graph paper, crayons and scissors.
- Make copies of the student page "Got You Covered!" (page 145).

Use:

1) Give each student three pieces of graph paper and a copy of the student page.

2) Go through the information on the student page together and work as a group to solve the area problems (except for the last problem).

3) Have the students show the areas of other figures by using crayons, graph paper and scissors. For example:

   Color a figure with an area of 10 cm².
   Show a figure with an area of 22 cm².
   Cut out a figure with an area of 18 cm².

4) Have the students draw around their feet (without shoes) on graph paper and then count squares to find the approximate area.

Measurement
Area

Got You Covered!

The area of this square is 1 square centimeter (1 cm²).

The area of this square is 9 square centimeters (9 cm²).

Find the area of the shaded figures below.

1. _____ cm².

2. _____ cm².

3. _____ cm².

4. _____ cm².

5. Color a figure with an area of 5 cm².

6. Color a figure with an area of 11 cm².

145

Student Page

Name _____

Caught With The Crumbs

The Cookie Gobbler got into the cookie jar and is going to eat these cookies. How big is each cookie? Find its area (in centimeters).

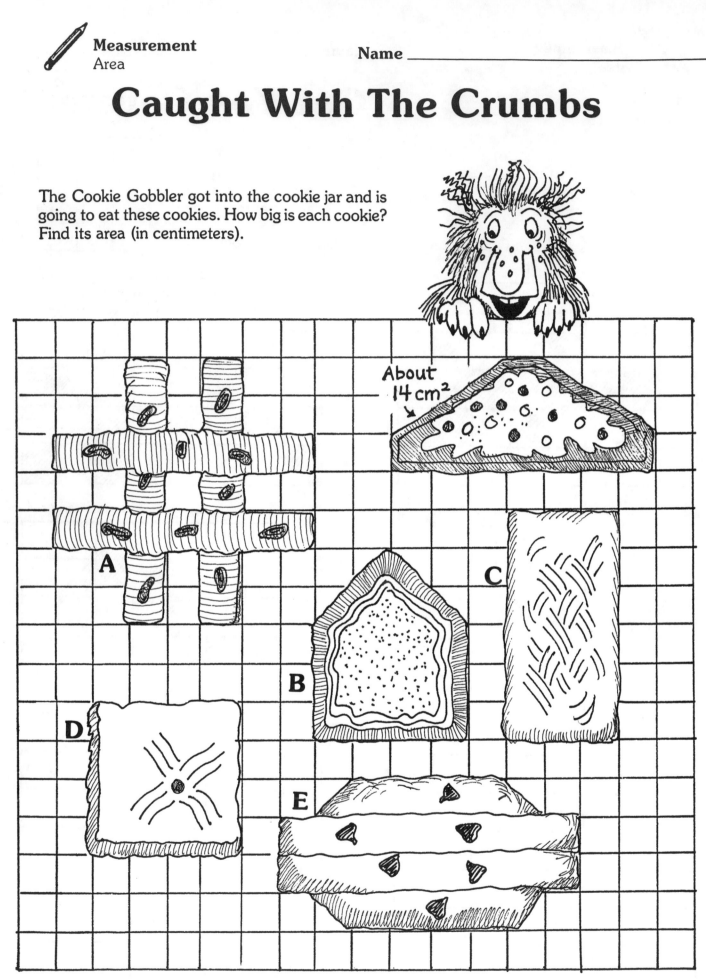

About 14 cm²

A

B

C

D

E

Name _____

Spying On Big Areas

A square meter (m²) is used to measure the area of large surfaces.

A square meter is a square that measures one meter on each side.

"Spy" on each of these objects and find its area. Each square represents one square meter.

1. _____ m²

2. _____ m²

3. _____ m²

4. _____ m²

Measurement
Volume

Cubes You Can Count On

Preparation:
- Make copies of the student page "The Cubic Centimeter" (page 149). If possible, use stiff paper for making copies to insure durability.
- Bring containers to class (cereal box, cracker box, lunch box, cake pan, etc.) which can be measured by filling them with cubic centimeters made by the students.
- Students will need scissors and tape.

Use:
1) Explain the concept of volume — finding out how much something holds. Tell the students that cubic units are used to measure volume.
2) Give the students time to make a few cubic centimeters using the pattern on page 149.
3) Work together to fill various containers and measure the volume of each. Have the students write each measurement correctly.

Name _____

The Cubic Centimeter

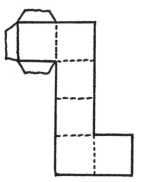

Follow the steps below to make a
cubic centimeter (cm³).
1. Cut on the solid lines.
2. Fold on the dotted lines.
3. Tape the tabs to make a cube.

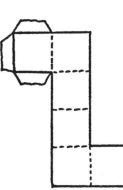

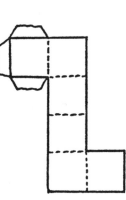

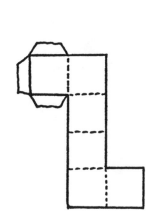

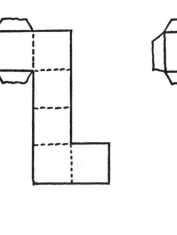

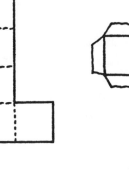

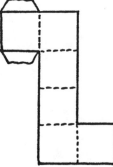

Student Page

Big Cubes For Big Spaces

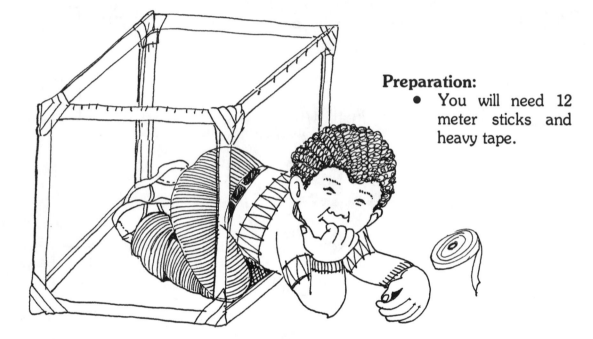

Preparation:
- You will need 12 meter sticks and heavy tape.

Use:

1) Let the students help you make a cubic meter for measuring spaces that are too large to be measured by cubic centimeters.

2) When the cube is finished, let students explore the size, shape, and inside so they may get the "feel" of a cubic meter. (You might try to see how many kids can fit inside the cube!)

3) Work together to find the volume of the classroom. Students will need to move the cube and determine:

   how many of the cubes it takes to cover the floor
   how many layers of cubes it would take to reach the ceiling

4) Help the students discover the easiest way to measure the volume of the room (measure and multiply: length x width x height of room).

Name _____

Hold Everything!

Each of these containers is full of cereal. Which one holds about:

A. 800 cm³? _____

C. 3000 cm³? _____

B. 600 cm³? _____

D. 1600 cm³? _____

Name _____

Outsmart Smarty-Cat

Smarty-cat thinks he knows which kind of unit to use to measure each of these objects. Do you?
Write length, area, or volume beside each object to show the correct unit of measurement.

You measure the length of something to find out how long it is.

You measure the area of something to find out how much space is covered.

You measure the volume of something to find out how much something holds.

1. What unit measures the amount of frosting needed to cover a cake?

2. What unit measures the amount of punch in a glass?

3. What unit measures the amount of water in a swimming pool?

4. What unit measures how long a belt is?

5. What unit measures the size of a quilt?

6. What unit measures the amount of water in a lake?

7. What unit measures the distance to school?

8. What unit measures the sand in a sandbox?

9. What unit tells how long each board is?

10. What unit measures the height of the fence?

11. What unit measures the amount of water in a tub?

12. What unit tells how long this jump rope is?

13. What unit tells how long this hose is?

Measurement
Liquid

Metric Lemonade

Preparation:

- Make a copy of the lemonade recipe on poster board.
- You will need:
  lemons
  water
  sugar
  large spoon
  ice
  sharp knife (for cutting lemons)
  2 gallon pitchers
  small paper cups
  liter measuring container
  as many "juicers" as available

Use:

1. Begin by having a small group of students squeeze lemons to collect one liter of lemon juice.
2. Have the students take turns measuring the ingredients and mixing them in a large pitcher.
3. Pour half of the lemonade into the other pitcher and add ice to both. Stir well and serve in paper cups.

METRIC LEMONADE
RECIPE:
3 Liters Water
1 Liter Lemon Juice
.5 Liters Sugar

Measurement
Mass

Name _____

A Weighty Matter

Mass is a measurement of the amount of matter in an object.

To measure small things, use a gram (g).
Measure heavier things with a kilogram (kg) which equals 1000 grams.
Measure very heavy things with a metric ton (t) which equals 1000 kilograms.

One gram is the mass of the water that would fill a cubic centimeter.

paper clip —
about 1 gram

nickel —
about 5 grams

candy bar — about
100 grams

large hamburger —
about 250 grams

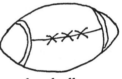

football —
about 500 grams

liter of water —
1 kilogram

desk dictionary —
about 6 kilograms

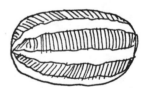

large watermelon —
about 20 kilograms

large car — about 1 ton

school bus — about 5 tons

What unit would you use to measure each item below?

1. an apple _____
2. a T.V. _____
3. an elephant _____

4. a bicycle _____
5. a baseball cap _____
6. a cupcake _____

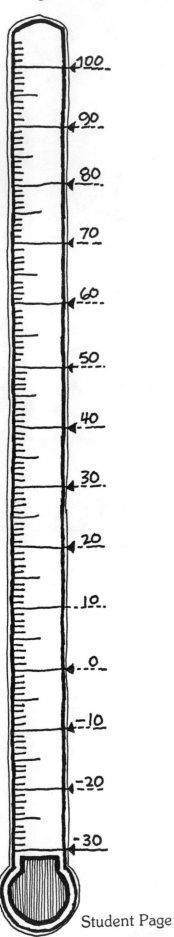

Name _____

Temperature Talk

Estimate how hot or cold each item below is. Use a centigrade temperature scale. Then draw a line to connect each picture to its temperature on the centigrade thermometer.

ESTIMATED TEMPERATURE

Time & Money

Time-Telling Tongues

Hee Hee Hee

Giggle, Giggle

That's 3 o'clock!

Preparation:

- All you need for this activity is a group of kids who love to stick out their tongues!

Use:

1) Have the students look carefully at the numbers on a clock to discover where each number is positioned.
2) Have the students stick out their tongues to show the position of 12 o'clock. Then have the students show the positions of other numbers.

The Human Clock

Preparation:

- Use chalk, string, or tape to make a huge circle on the classroom floor, on the playground, or on the grass. Number the circle to make it look like a clock.

Use:

Students who are just beginning to tell time will learn about clocks much faster if their bodies are involved in the process. This is a way to assure that students really "get a feel" for the changing positions of a clock's hands.

1) Choose two students to be the hands of the clock (preferably one a little taller than the other).

2) Dictate times and have the two students position themselves to show the time.

3) Let the two students agree on a time to show and have the other students read the time.

Teacher Page

Just In Time

Preparation:
- Have a supply of large paper plates and art supplies for making the plates into clocks (construction paper, staplers, glue, markers, scissors).

Use:
1) Let the students talk about interesting clocks they've seen.
2) Allow time for the students to design and make clocks (which show specific times). Encourage variety.
3) Number each clock and hang them around the room. Work together to practice reading and writing times on all of the clocks.
4) For more practice, give each student a copy of the student page "It's About Time" (page 161).

Time & Money
Telling Time

Name _____

It's About Time

1. Which clock shows nine-thirty? _____
2. Which clock shows noon? _____
3. Which clock shows ten after three? _____
4. Which clock shows six-twenty? _____

5. What time does clock B show? _____
6. What time does clock G show? _____
7. What time does clock D show? _____
8. What time does clock H show? _____

THE TIME IS: 6:20

2:51

How About A Date?

Preparation:
- You will need last year's calendar, this year's calendar, next year's calendar, and a calendar for each pair of students.

Use:

1) Work with the students to do "calendar calculations." Ask such questions as those below. Let the students discuss the questions and determine answers orally.

What will the date be one month and three days from now?

What was the date five weeks ago?

How long is it until St. Patrick's Day?

What will the date be 37 days from now?

How many days are left until Christmas vacation begins?

Which is farther away, March 6 or 66 days from now?

2) Give the students copies of the student page "Help From Your Calendar" (page 163) and let students work in pairs to answer the questions. (Each pair of students will need a calendar.)

Name _____

Help From Your Calendar

1. I fell off my skateboard and broke my leg today. I have to wear this cast for 10 weeks. On what date will the cast be removed?

   _____

2. I turned eight just five months and three weeks ago. When was my birthday?

   _____

3. I have a great costume for Halloween. How many months and days are left until I can wear it?

   _____ months _____ days

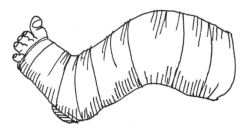

4. I told my little brother that he'd turn into a frog in seven weeks and two days. He believes me! On what date will he find out if I'm right?

   _____

Student Page

The Minute Minder

Maxie Minute Minder knows that there are 60 minutes in an hour and 30 minutes in half an hour.

Solve these problems faster than Maxie!

Only 6 hours and 15 minutes to go.

A. How many minutes are there in two hours?

_____

B. How many minutes are there in an hour and a half?

_____

C. How many hours is 180 minutes?

_____

D. How many minutes are there in 10 hours?

_____

E. How many hours is 45 minutes?

_____

Name _____

Taco Stop

Determine how much each customer will spend.

Taco.................... .75
Taco Supper................1.50
Nachos 1.25
Burrito .... .90
Taco Salad 2.00
Soda Pop .... .50
Milk......... .40 ; Tums......10

Missy Mouse

1 Taco

1 Tums

Molly Moo

24 Tacos

Harry Hound

4 Taco Suppers
1 Burrito
1 Milk

Brian Bear

1 Nachos
1 Burrito
1 Taco
1 Taco Supper
1 Taco Salad
6 Soda Pops
25 Tums

Shopping Wagon

Preparation:

- Bring a wagon or cart to class.
- Have the students bring "good junk" to put in the wagon (see example).

Use:

1) Set a price for each item that the students brought. (Because the items are not new, talk about fair "garage sale" prices.) Label each item with a price.
2) Practice adding the cost of any two or more items.
3) Give each student a copy of the student page "My Good Junk Shopping List" (page 167). Have the students choose and calculate the imaginary costs of their choices.

Name _____

My Good Junk Shopping List

Choose four things from the good junk cart. Write the name of each item and its price below.

	Item	Price
1)	_____	$ __ __ . __ __
2)	_____	$ __ __ . __ __
3)	_____	$ __ __ . __ __
4)	_____	$ __ __ . __ __

Now add the prices. How much will you spend to buy all four items?

Total $ _____

167   Student Page

Name _____

Who Has The Most?

ROBERTA
6 Dimes
4 Nickels
2 Pennies

GORDON
1 Quarter
1 Dime
1 Nickel
1 Penny

Which shopper has the most money?

PAM
3 Quarters
3 Pennies

CARL
7 Nickels
1 Dime

BERTHA
1 Quarter
5 Dimes
2 Nickels

ELMO
2 Quarters
1 Dime
1 Penny

Come on, Cough it up, Elmo.

168

Answer on page 240.

Put It In The Bank

8¢

40¢

37¢

26¢

16¢

Cut a slit in each piggy bank.

Cut out all of the coins. Then put the correct amount of money into each bank.

169

The Amazing Dollar

Myrtle Magician can "make" a dollar like this.

Samantha can "make" a dollar like this.

TEN DIMES

Adam can "make" a dollar like this.

THREE QUARTERS, FIVE NICKELS

Can you think of two other ways to "make" a dollar? You may use quarters, dimes, nickels, and pennies — but no dollars!

Draw two ways to make a dollar below.

Billions Of Bubbles

Billions Of Bubbles

Julie	O O O O O
Dustin	O O O
Roberto	O O O O
Danielle	O O
Adam	O O O O O O
David	O O O O
Franklin	O O O
Marika	O O O O O O O
Benson	O O O O O O
Jenna	O O
Sara	O O O O O O O O O O
Wally	O O O O O
Susan	O O O O O O
Angie	O O O O
Jeff	O O O
Mary	O O O O O O

O = 10 Bubbles

Preparation:
- Make bubbles by combining one part glycerine with 10 parts liquid dish washing soap. Divide this mixture among the students by pouring it into individual paper cups.
- Straws cut diagonally or pipe cleaner circles make good bubble blowing instruments. You will need plenty of paper towels and newspaper.

Use:
1) Make copies of the student page "Chicken Pox Checkup" (page 173) and use it to explain pictographs to the students. Give the students time to answer the questions.
2) Give each student a cup of bubble mixture and a blowing instrument. Tell the students that they will have three minutes to blow bubbles and that they must count the bubbles as they blow them. (If they blow slowly, counting will be much easier.)
3) After the three minutes are up, make a list on the board of the total number of bubbles blown by each student.
4) Work together to make a pictograph showing the results of the counting experiment.

Chicken Pox Checkup

Read the graph below to find out how many students in each grade at Washington School have had chicken pox.

Grade   Chicken Pox at Washington School

K	🐔🐔🐔
1st	🐔🐔🐔
2nd	🐔🐔🐔🐔
3rd	🐔🐔🐔🐔🐔🐔🐔
4th	🐔🐔🐔🐔🐔🐔🐔
5th	🐔🐔🐔🐔🐔🐔🐔🐔🐔

One chicken = 10 kids with chicken pox.

How many kids have had chicken pox in

kindergarten? _____   first grade? _____

second grade? _____   third grade? _____

fourth grade? _____   fifth grade? _____

Name _____

No Spinach, Thank You

What food do you *dislike* the most: spinach, ice cream, olives, liver, egg salad, or licorice?

Ask your classmates this question. Then make a graph to show what foods they dislike most.

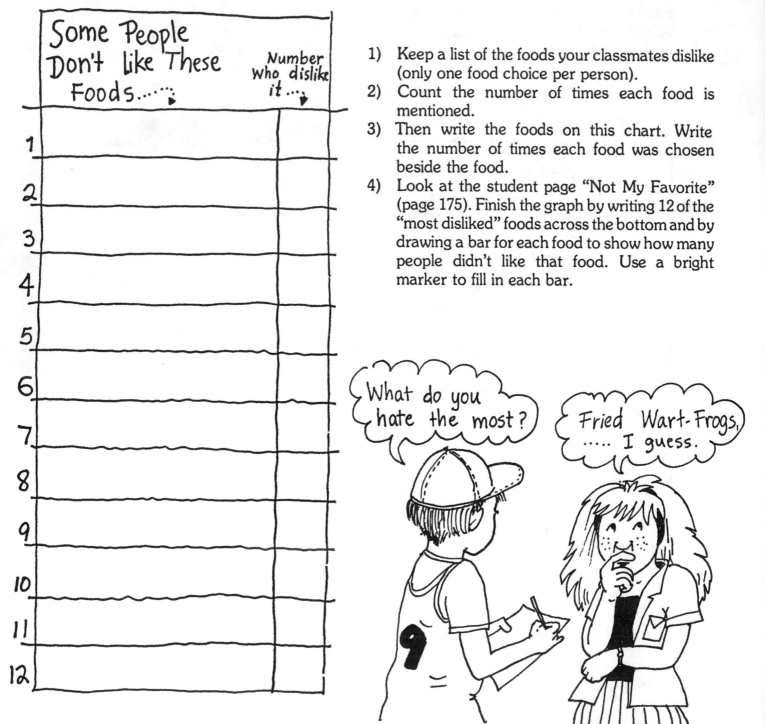

Some People Don't like These Foods......

Number who dislike it ...

1
2
3
4
5
6
7
8
9
10
11
12

1) Keep a list of the foods your classmates dislike (only one food choice per person).

2) Count the number of times each food is mentioned.

3) Then write the foods on this chart. Write the number of times each food was chosen beside the food.

4) Look at the student page "Not My Favorite" (page 175). Finish the graph by writing 12 of the "most disliked" foods across the bottom and by drawing a bar for each food to show how many people didn't like that food. Use a bright marker to fill in each bar.

What do you hate the most?

Fried Wart-Frogs, ... I guess.

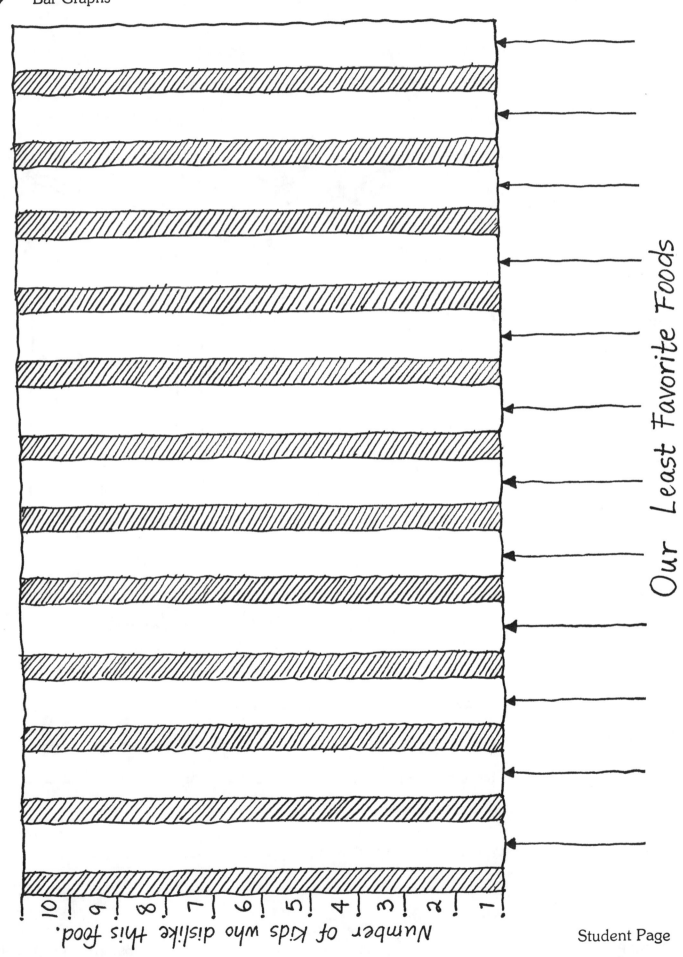

Not My Favorite

Our Least Favorite Foods

10 9 8 7 6 5 4 3 2 1

Number of kids who dislike this food.

Name _____

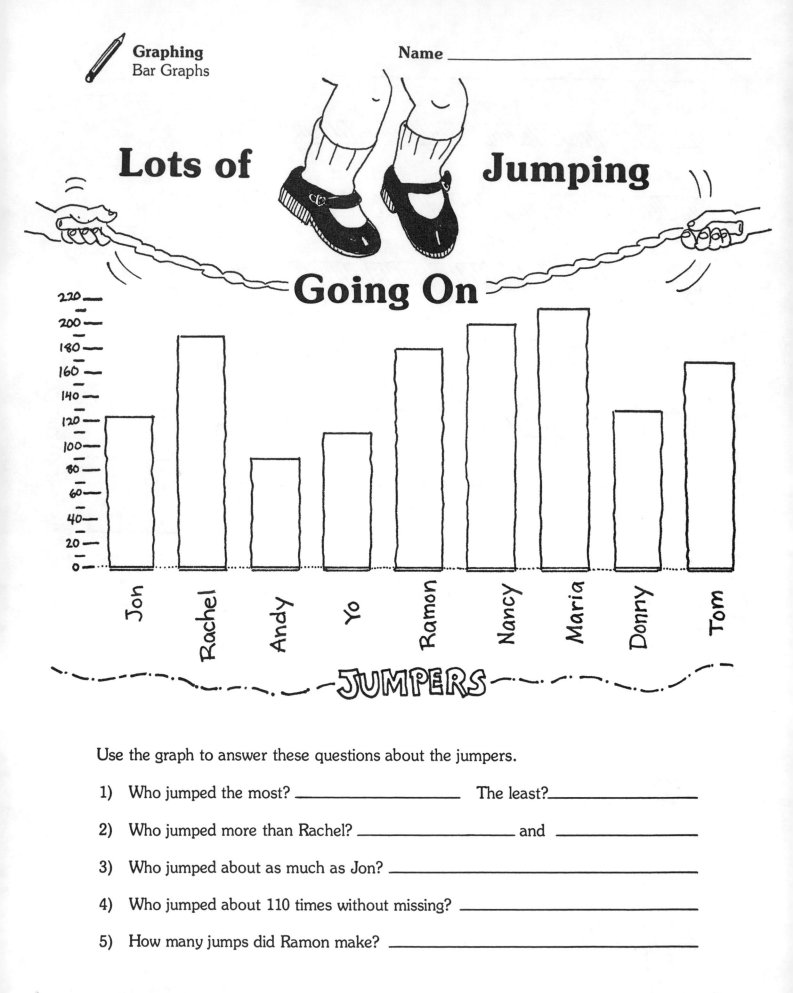

Lots of Jumping Going On

220
200
180
160
140
120
100
80
60
40
20
0

Jon Rachel Andy Yo Ramon Nancy Maria Donny Tom

JUMPERS

Use the graph to answer these questions about the jumpers.

1) Who jumped the most? _____ The least? _____

2) Who jumped more than Rachel? _____ and _____

3) Who jumped about as much as Jon? _____

4) Who jumped about 110 times without missing? _____

5) How many jumps did Ramon make? _____

Student Page

176

Answers on page 240.

Graphing
Line Graphs

Name _____

Leaping Leapfrogs!

Teresa Toad and Ferdinand Frog had a week-long jumping contest. Read the graph and find out how they did!

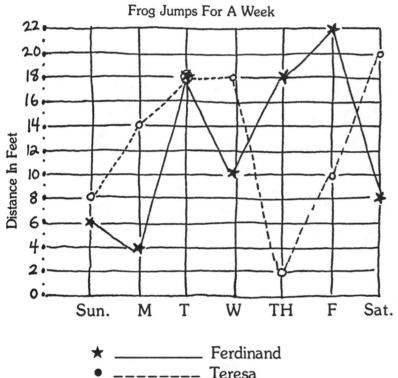

Frog Jumps For A Week

Distance In Feet

22
20
18
16
14
12
10
8
6
4
2
0

Sun.   M   T   W   TH   F   Sat.

★ _____ Ferdinand
● - - - - - - Teresa

1) How many total feet had Ferdinand jumped after Monday and Tuesday? ___

2) What was the difference between the longest and shortest jump? _____

3) Who jumped the farthest on Wednesday? _____

4) On which day did both frogs jump the same distance? _____

5) What was Ferdinand's worst day? _____

6) What was Teresa's worst day? _____

7) How far did Teresa jump on Friday? _____

Name _____

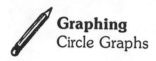

The School Day Target

A circle graph gives you information about the parts of a whole.

This one shows how Isaac's school day is spent.

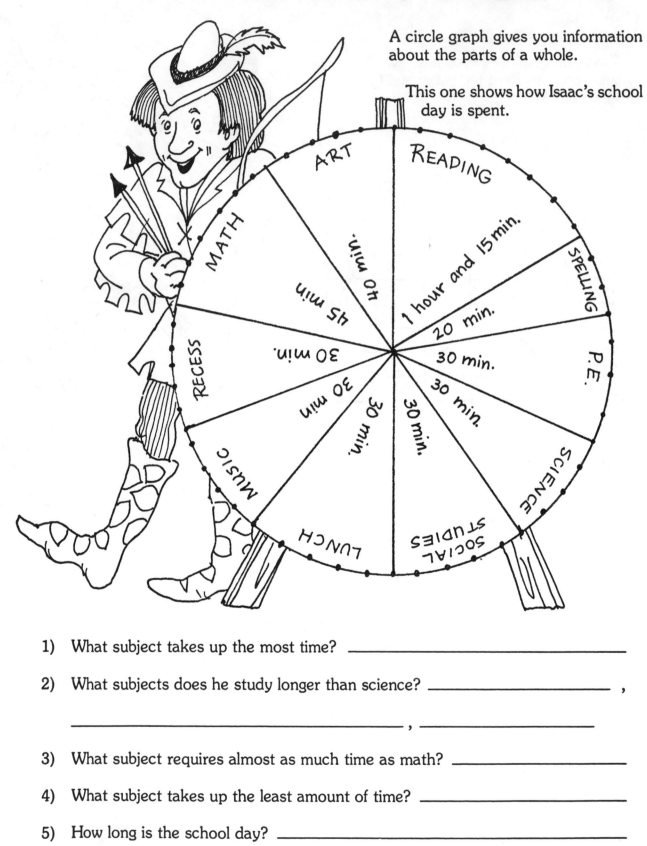

1) What subject takes up the most time? _____

2) What subjects does he study longer than science? _____ ,

_____ , _____

3) What subject requires almost as much time as math? _____

4) What subject takes up the least amount of time? _____

5) How long is the school day? _____

Over & Up

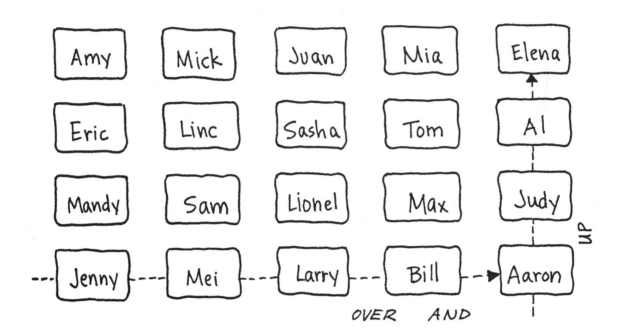

Preparation:
- Arrange the classroom desks in even rows to form a simulated grid.

Use:

When young students are beginning to learn the concept of locating a point by graphing coordinates, it helps for the students to *be* the coordinates.

1) Tell the students that you are going to use a special method to locate each one of their desks. Identify the number of each vertical row and each horizontal row.

2) Locate one of the students. For example, Juan is three rows *over* and four rows *up*. Let the students help to locate others. Tell students to find the *over* location before the *up* location. Write Juan's location on the board (3,4).

3) Explain that the word coordinates means "a pair of numbers that gives the location of something on a grid." (A grid is a pattern of horizontal and vertical rows.)

4) Continue locating students and writing the coordinates for each. (Always write the coordinates in parentheses.)

5) Use the following five student pages for more practice with coordinates.

Teacher Page

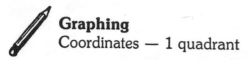

Name _____

Track Down The Toys

When you read or write coordinates, always go *over* first and then *up*.
Use coordinates to find the toys on the graph below.

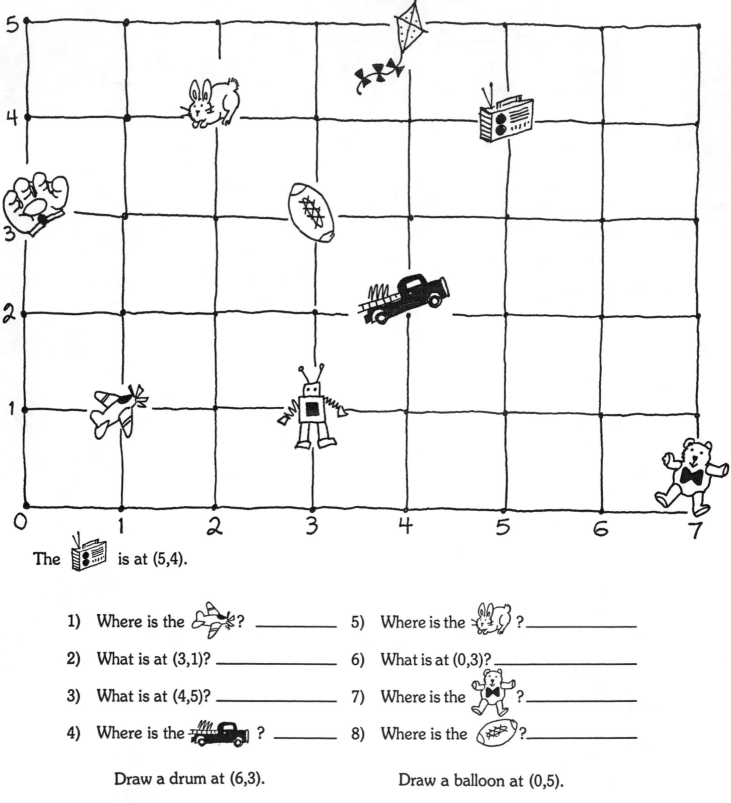

The 📻 is at (5,4).

1) Where is the ✈? _____   5) Where is the 🐰? _____

2) What is at (3,1)? _____   6) What is at (0,3)? _____

3) What is at (4,5)? _____   7) Where is the 🧸? _____

4) Where is the 🚚? _____   8) Where is the 🏈? _____

Draw a drum at (6,3).   Draw a balloon at (0,5).

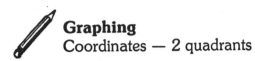

Graphing
Coordinates — 2 quadrants

Name _____

Letter Perfect

When there are two sections (quadrants) on a grid, always begin counting from zero.

The B is at (-1,3). That's -1 *over* and 3 *up*.

Graph each pair of coordinates below to spell a secret message.

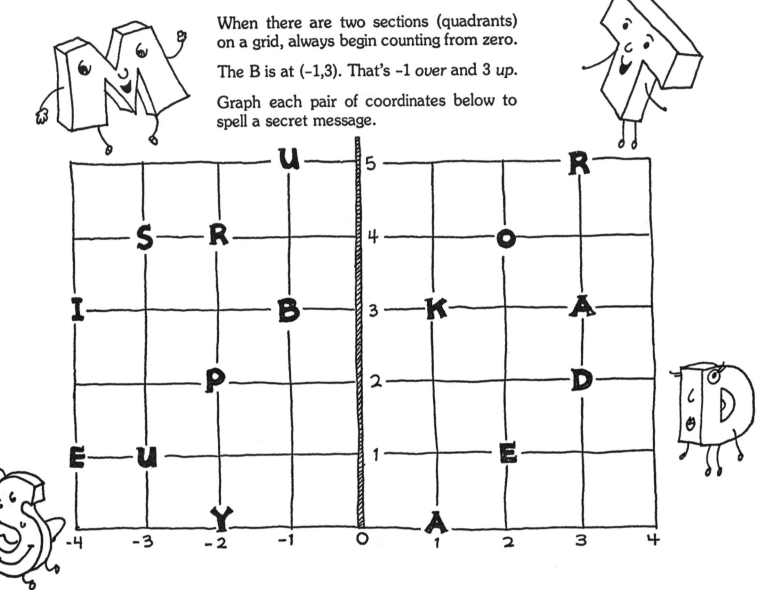

__ __ __   __ __ __   __

(-2,0) (2,4) (-1,5)   (3,3) (-2,4) (-4,1)   (1,0)

!

__ __ __ __ __   __ __ __

(-3,4) (-3,1) (-2,2) (2,1) (3,5)   (1,3) (-4,3) (3,2)

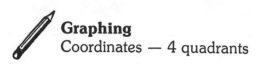
Once Upon A Picnic

These picnickers seem to be missing some things. Use the picnic tablecloth grid on the next page to help find their food.

1) Where is the ?   _____

2) Where is the 🥕 ?   _____

3) What is at (–2, –3)?   _____

4) Where is the 🍞 ?   _____

5) What dessert is at (–3, 3)?   _____

6) Where is the 🍉 ?   _____

Draw an ant at (4,–5).

Draw a salt shaker at (4,0).

Draw an ice cream cone at (–2, –5).

Draw a soda bottle at (–2,1).

Join The Picnic

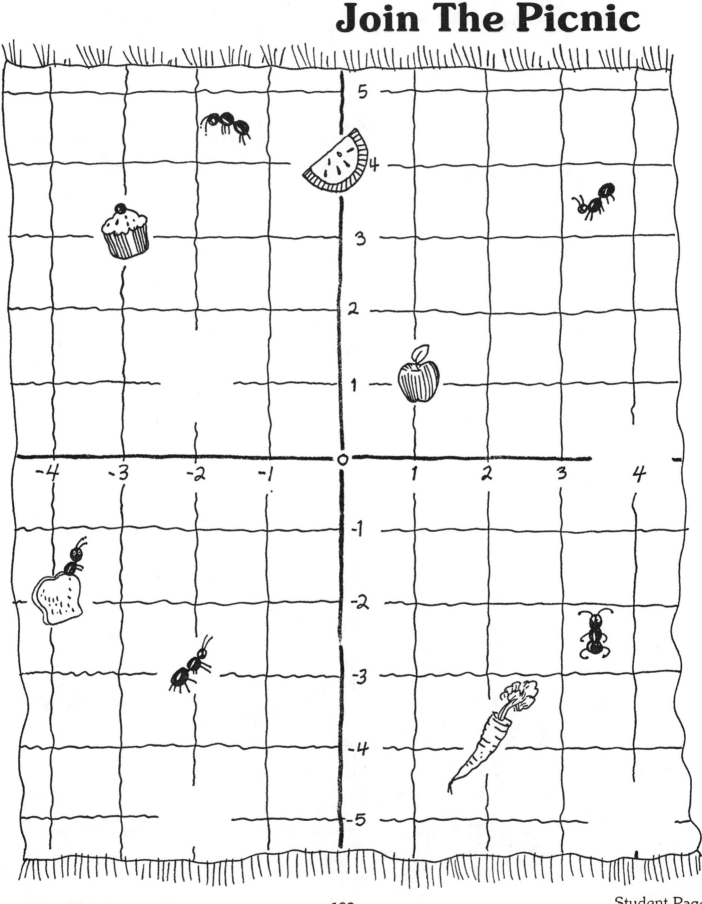

Bunny On The Lookout

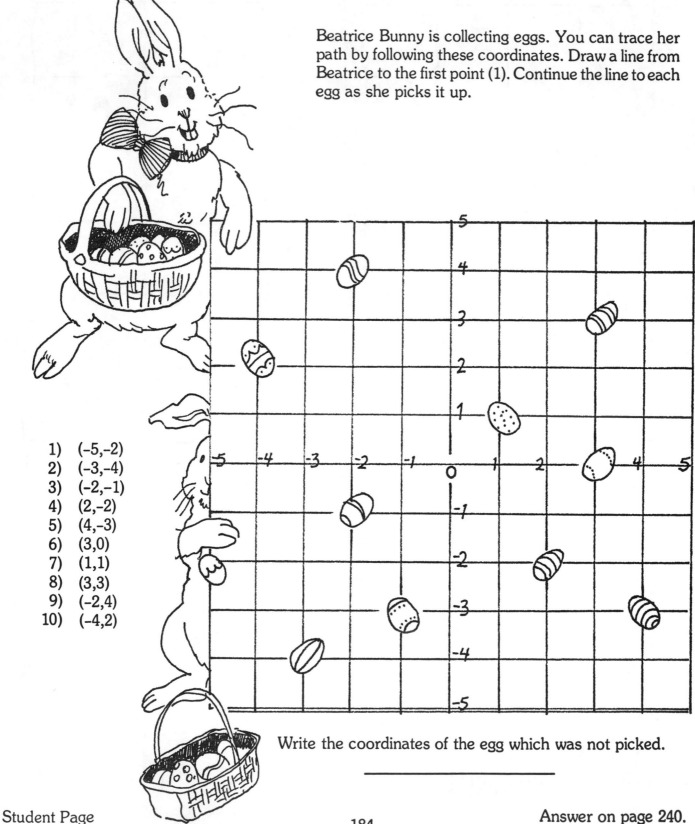

Beatrice Bunny is collecting eggs. You can trace her path by following these coordinates. Draw a line from Beatrice to the first point (1). Continue the line to each egg as she picks it up.

1) (–5,–2)
2) (–3,–4)
3) (–2,–1)
4) (2,–2)
5) (4,–3)
6) (3,0)
7) (1,1)
8) (3,3)
9) (–2,4)
10) (–4,2)

Write the coordinates of the egg which was not picked.

_____

Problem Solving

Which Ones Will Balance?

If the problems on both ends of the teeter totter have the same answer, then the teeter totter will balance.

Which ones will balance?

Name _____

Monstrous Problems

These monsters have problems! Can you help?
Write a number problem for each question and
then find the answer.
Color the picture.

1) Altogether the monsters ate
246 cookies. Each monster ate
the same number of cookies.
How many cookies did each
monster eat?

2) The monsters with claws
wanted to go roller-skating
with the monsters with tails.
How many pairs of skates
would they need?

3) All of the monsters who are
not wearing clothes went to
buy some. Each monster
bought five items. How many
total items were bought?

Name _____

Which Witch?

Each witch does one math process.

Look at the symbols to determine which witch adds, which witch subtracts, which witch multiplies, and which witch divides.

Read each problem below and on the next page. Decide whether the problem requires addition, subtraction, multiplication or division. Tell which witch can solve the problem.

1) If a bug can crawl two feet a day and it crawls for 16 days, how far will it get?

2) John had 100 jellybeans. His turtle swallowed 17. How many are left?

Name _____

8) Nancy did 113 cartwheels on Monday, 55 on Tuesday, and 79 on Wednesday. How many cartwheels did she do in all?

3) Gregory Giant was 62 feet tall last year. He grew three feet this year. How tall is he now?

4) Four friends decided to count their shoes. J.R. has nine pair, Penny has 12 pair, Jane has eight pair, and Bo has 10 pair. How many pairs of shoes do the friends have altogether?

5) A family of zebras slept six hours a day for one week. How many hours did they sleep that week?

6) Melissa ate pizza 109 days last year. The year had 365 days. How many days did she not eat pizza?

9) All of the 27 kids in Mrs. French's second grade class lost three teeth last year. How many total teeth were lost?

7) A rocket shot up to 27,955 feet and then fell to 13,888 feet before the parachute opened. How far was the fall before the parachute opened?

10) At a pie eating contest, Homer Hungry ate 16 pies. He ate four times as many pies as Gregory Gulp. How many pies did Gregory eat?

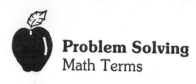
A Puzzle For Ears

Preparation:
- Make a copy of the student page "Puzzle Me" (page 191) for each student.

Use:
1) Read the following clues one at a time to the students.
2) After each clue is given, allow time for the students to think of a math term which fits the clue and the puzzle space.

Clues

Down

1. The place to the left of the tens place.
2) A numeral that shows part of a whole.
3. The process of finding the length, area, weight, or volume.
5. A geometric figure with six square faces.
7. A figure with three sides.
10. What you do to find the difference between two numbers.
11. The answer in a multiplication problem.

Across

4. A four-sided figure with four right angles.
5. A tool for drawing circles.
6. The opposite of add.
8. A small unit in the metric system for measuring length.
9. A unit used for measuring temperature.
12. The top number of a fraction.
13. What you do to find the sum of two numbers.
14. A polygon with four equal sides and four right angles.

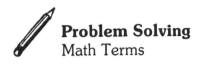

Puzzle Me

Something's Popping

Preparation:
- You will need a large bag of popped popcorn, a jar of unpopped popcorn, and assorted containers such as paper cups, a mixing bowl, a gallon jar, etc.
- Fill several containers (of differing sizes) with popped popcorn.

Use:
1) Talk about the process of estimating. Use one container of popcorn as an example. Work as a class to estimate the number of kernels of popcorn in the container.
2) Have the students work in small groups to estimate the number of popped popcorn kernels in other containers. Then let the students count the kernels to check their estimates.
3) Try estimation activities with unpopped kernels, too.
4) Give each student a paper cup of popped popcorn. Have the students make estimates of the number of kernels before counting and eating the popcorn!

Teacher Page

Name _____

Space Search

Solve the problems and color the spaces as directed by the code below to find out what is "lost in space."

15 - yellow   20 - purple   16 - red   9 - orange   12 - blue

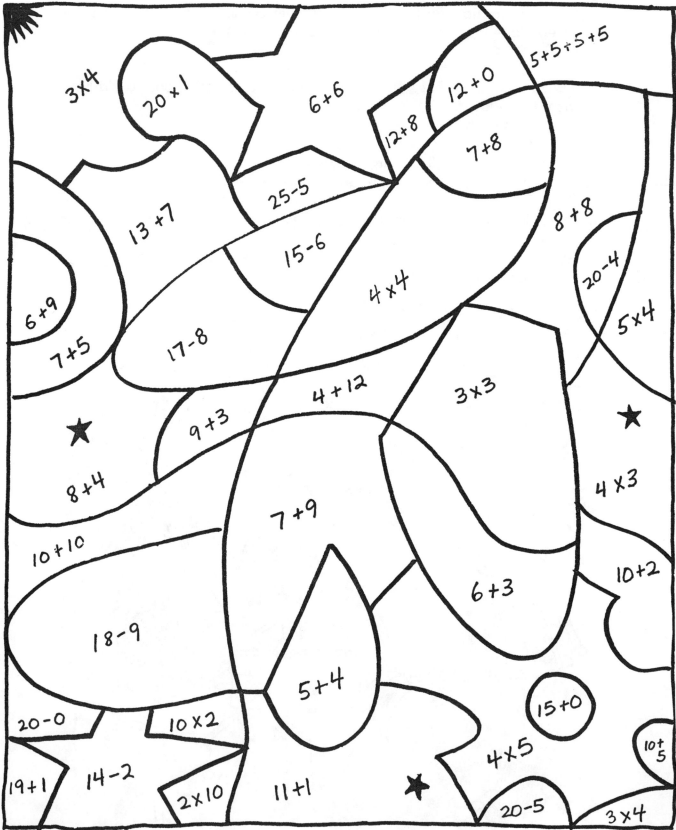

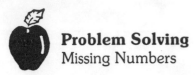

Mystery Numbers

Preparation:
- Make preparations for the "Mystery Number Game" by thinking of clues for several mystery numbers (see the example below).

Use:
1) Tell the students that you have a mystery number that you would like them to discover.
2) Give clues such as:

   It's smaller than 15 but larger than 3.
   It is half of a number that is larger than 10.

3) The students may take turns guessing the mystery number after each clue is given.
4) Repeat this activity with several mystery numbers. Then let the students take turns choosing the mystery number.

Name _____

License Plate Math

Use the numbers on these license plates to make
your own math problems!

Example:

$$716 \atop + 598$$ $$123 \atop \times 002$$

M0123

444 PU

EZ 716

598 BC

340 ACRE

002 TU

195

Student Page

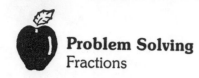
Kid Problems

Preparation:

- All that you need for this activity is a group of kids!

Use:

1) Review the structure of a fraction.

   Remind students that: the numerator tells how many of the parts of a unit (whole) are taken

   the denominator tells how many parts make a complete unit (whole)

2) Use fractions to name groups of students. For example:

   How many students in this class are eight years old?
   How many students have a birthday in October?
   How many students bought a lunch today?
   How many students have sisters?
   How many students are wearing sweaters?

3) Give each student a copy of the student page "From The Lineup" (page 197). Have the students write a fractional answer for each problem.

Name _____

From The Lineup

1. How many kids have braids? _____
2. How many kids are wearing the letter "G"? _____
3. How many kids are wearing the letter "B"? _____
4. How many kids have pompoms? _____
5. How many kids have freckles? _____
6. How many kids have shoes with untied laces? _____
7. How many kids have a hand or hands above their heads? _____
8. How many kids are sitting? _____
9. How many kids are standing? _____
10. How many kids have striped pants? _____

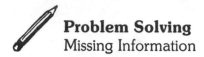
What's Missing?

Wally is missing several socks. Each of these problems is "missing something," too. What do you need to know before you can solve each problem?

1. There are seven striped socks and some other socks. How many socks are there in all?

   _____

2. There are four drawers in all. One drawer contains socks.

   _____

3. There are eight rooms in Wally's house. How many bedrooms are there?

   _____

4. Wally found four socks today. He found four socks yesterday.

   _____

5. Wally looked for missing socks for 10 minutes today. How long has he looked for socks all week?

   _____

6. Wally's mom has reminded him to put pairs of socks together ever since he was four years old. How long has she been reminding Wally to do this?

   _____

All In The Neighborhood

On this map, 1 centimeter equals 10 meters.

1) Which neighbor lives about 20 meters from Ty?
2) How far is it from Julie's house to Sam's house?
3) Who would walk the farthest from home to the playground?
4) How far does the teacher walk to school?
5) Would Sasha walk more than 200 meters to the market?
6) What's the shortest way for Sam to get to the fire station?
7) Tell how far Jason and Craig live from the library.

Answers on page 240.

199

Student Page

Name _____

Who Won The Game?

Shakers	Points	Fouls	Stompers	Points	Fouls
Adams	7	1	Martin	5	1
Thomas	22	5	James	0	0
Gomez	3	1	Titus	3	0
Williams	9	0	Black	7	2
Nicholson	0	2	Jefferson	7	3
Chang	23	3	Olsen	14	2
Winters	4	4	Goldstein	11	4
Barnes	6	0	Grabowitz	26	3
Threefeathers	3	2	Reilly	4	1
Romero	16	1	Papadapolus	8	0

The basketball game is over.
Here are the scores for each player.

1. Which team won? _____

_____

2. Which team had the most fouls?

_____

3. What was the final score?

_____

Name _____

World Travelers

The Globe family has spent the summer visiting some interesting places. This is where they went.

From home to Dishpanland Park	489 miles
From Dishpanland Park to Hitop Mountains	370 miles
From Hitop Mountains to Dry Bones Desert	900 miles
From Dry Bones Desert to Dillydally Lake	760 miles
From Dillydally Lake to Crocodile Creek	254 miles
From Crocodile Creek to Cowboy Corral	100 miles
From Cowboy Corral back home again	50 miles

A. How far did they travel from home
to Dillydally Lake?   _____

B. How much farther did they travel on their longest
day of travel than on their shortest day?   _____

C. How far was Cowboy Corral from their home?   _____

D. How many miles did they travel in all?   _____

Name _____

Long Distance Dialings

Use the information about the phone calls below to answer the questions on page 203.

Jenny called her Aunt in Miami.	5 minutes	$ 2.76
Mr. McGraw ordered lobsters from Maine.	3 minutes	$ 2.10
Papa Giazoni wished a happy birthday to his brother in Italy.	10 minutes	$17.15
Mrs. Chun called Seattle to tell friends about the new baby.	15 minutes	$ 8.15
Ted called his mom in Concord, California from camp.	4 minutes	$ 1.13
Steven's dad called him from New Hampshire while on a business trip.	12 minutes	$ 5.77

TELEPHONE BOOK

Hello! Hello! Is Anybody there?

Name _____

1) How much total money was spent on the six phone calls? _____

2) Papa Giazoni spent how much more money than Jenny? _____

3) How much time was spent on the six phone calls in all? _____

4) Mrs. Chun talked how much longer than Ted? _____

5) Who spent more money, Mr. McGraw or Steven's dad and by how much? _____

6) Mrs. Chun spent how much more money than Mr. McGraw? _____

IT'S YOUR AUNT IN TANZANIA!

Thanks

I'll Have Chocolate Fudge

How many different single-dip
cones could you get at this ice cream parlor?

List each one below.

How many different sundaes (1 dip of ice cream with one topping) could you order?
List each one below.

MATH TOOLS & TREASURES

SKILLS THAT MAKE A MATH WHIZ

Numeration
____ Recognizing that numerals name numbers
____ Associating word names with corresponding numerals
____ Reading and writing numerals with one and six digits
____ Associating numerals with intervals along a number line
____ Identifying place value for one, two, and three-digit numerals
____ Identifying place value for four, five, and six-digit numerals
____ Identifying place value for millions
____ Expressing numerals in expanded notation
____ Renaming tens as ones
____ Renaming hundreds as tens
____ Renaming thousands as hundreds
____ Renaming ten thousands as thousands, hundred thousands as ten thousands, and millions as hundred thousands
____ Reading and expressing numerals using an abacus
____ Distinguishing between numerals having the same digits in different positions
____ Identifying positive and negative integers
____ Reading and writing Roman numerals
____ Devising an original numeration system based on 10
____ Experimenting with a non-decimal based numeration system

Sets
____ Classifying objects into sets
____ Associating numerals and number words with sets of numbers
____ Writing numerals to correspond with sets
____ Associating zero with an empty set
____ Separating sets into subsets
____ Grouping items into sets of two, five, and ten
____ Given two sets, identifying which is greater
____ Identifying equivalent sets
____ Identifying non-equivalent sets
____ Arranging sets in order of size
____ Finding the union of two or more sets
____ Reading and writing large numbers: millions, billions, trillions
____ Reading exponential numbers

Number Concepts

- ____ Identifying even and odd numbers
- ____ Identifying prime and composite numbers
- ____ Ordering whole numbers
- ____ Putting positive and negative integers in sequence
- ____ Recognizing ordinal positions (first through tenth)
- ____ Recognizing a whole as greater than any of its parts
- ____ Understanding the value of zero
- ____ Understanding and using the concept of equal
- ____ Understanding and using the concept of inequality
- ____ Reading and writing sentences which name whole numbers
- ____ Comparing numbers and identifying which is less and which is greater
- ____ Reading and writing sentences using the symbols < and >
- ____ Completing sequences of whole numbers
- ____ Recognizing number patterns
- ____ Rounding whole numbers to the nearest 10, 100, and 1000
- ____ Rounding whole numbers to the nearest 10,000, 100,000 and 1,000,000

Addition and Subtraction of Whole Numbers

- ____ Understanding and using the symbols + and –
- ____ Learning sums through 20
- ____ Learning differences through 20
- ____ Using the terms addend, sum, and difference
- ____ Understanding the inverse relationship between addition and subtraction
- ____ Learning fact families through 20
- ____ Recognizing zero as the identity element for addition
- ____ Using the commutative property for addition
- ____ Finding the missing addend in addition sentences
- ____ Using a number line to find sums and differences
- ____ Using the associative property for addition
- ____ Adding and subtracting vertically
- ____ Finding sums and differences with two, three, four, five and six-digit numerals
- ____ Estimating sums and differences
- ____ Checking addition problems using subtraction
- ____ Checking subtraction problems using addition
- ____ Adding by renaming
- ____ Subtracting by renaming
- ____ Adding long columns of numbers
- ____ Adding and subtracting with more than six digits
- ____ Writing related addition and subtraction sentences
- ____ Solving word problems using addition and subtraction facts

Multiplication and Division of Whole Numbers

____ Grouping objects into equivalent sets
____ Separating objects into equivalent subsets
____ Seeing multiplication as the joining of equivalent sets
____ Seeing multiplication as repeated addition
____ Seeing division as the separation of sets into equivalent subsets
____ Seeing division as repeated subtraction
____ Recognizing the inverse relationship of multiplication and division
____ Writing multiplication sentences for numbers in sets
____ Writing division sentences for numbers in subsets
____ Learning multiplication facts for factors through 10
____ Learning fact families for products through 100
____ Using the terms factor and product
____ Solving multiplication and division problems using the number line
____ Recognizing "one" as the identity element in multiplication
____ Using the commutative property for multiplication
____ Discovering the role of zero in multiplication and division
____ Using the associative property for multiplication
____ Writing and solving word problems using multiplication and division facts through 100
____ Multiplying and dividing by 10 and multiples of 10
____ Identifying factors of a number
____ Identifying prime factors of a number
____ Completing prime factorization using factor trees
____ Finding the greatest common factor of two numbers
____ Finding the least common multiple of two numbers
____ Estimating products and quotients
____ Multiplying numbers by a one-digit number
____ Multiplying by two, three, and four-digit numbers
____ Using the distributive property of multiplication over addition
____ Using multiplication to write exponential numbers in expanded notation and writing them in full amounts
____ Dividing by one-digit divisors
____ Completing division problems that have remainders
____ Using the terms divisor, quotient, and remainder
____ Dividing by two, three, and higher-digit divisors
____ Checking division problems using multiplication
____ Finding averages
____ Determining if numbers are divisible by 2, 3, 4, 5, and 10

Fractions

____ Identifying halves, fourths, and thirds
____ Recognizing that two halves, three thirds, four fourths, etc. make a whole

_____ Using fractions to name parts of sets
_____ Identifying and understanding the significance of the numerator of a fraction
_____ Identifying and understanding the significance of the denominator of a fraction
_____ Reading and writing fractions
_____ Adding and subtracting like fractions
_____ Finding the least common multiple for the denominators of two unlike fractions
_____ Rewriting unlike fractions as like fractions
_____ Adding and subtracting unlike fractions
_____ Finding the greatest common factor for the numerator and denominator of a fraction
_____ Identifying fractions that are not in lowest terms
_____ Rewriting a fraction in lowest terms
_____ Identifying equivalent fractions
_____ Identifying improper fractions
_____ Determining which of two fractions is greater or less
_____ Putting a group of unlike fractions in order
_____ Identifying mixed fractional numerals
_____ Rewriting improper fractions as mixed numerals
_____ Rewriting mixed numerals as improper fractions
_____ Multiplying fractions
_____ Dividing fractions using the reciprocal method
_____ Dividing mixed numerals
_____ Using fractions to name ratios
_____ Expressing fractional numerals as decimals

Decimals
_____ Using dollar signs and decimal points to write money amounts
_____ Adding and subtracting with money
_____ Multiplying and dividing with money
_____ Understanding that the decimal system is based on 10s
_____ Understanding the place value of each place to the right of the decimal point
_____ Writing decimals to three places to the right of the decimal point
_____ Writing decimals more than three places to the right of the decimal point
_____ Writing mixed decimal numerals
_____ Learning to place the decimal point in products
_____ Learning to place the decimal point in quotients
_____ Adding, subtracting, multiplying, and dividing decimals
_____ Expressing decimal numerals as fractions
_____ Expressing decimals as percents

Measurement

___ Comparing lengths and sizes
___ Understanding the concepts smaller, larger, greater, less and more
___ Naming days of the week and months of the year
___ Telling time to the nearest hour and half hour
___ Telling time to the nearest minute and the nearest second
___ Knowing the number of: seconds in a minute, minutes in an hour, hours in a day, days in a week, weeks in a year, days in a month, etc.
___ Measuring length using U.S. and metric measures
___ Comparing weights of two or more objects
___ Measuring liquid capacity using U.S. and metric measures
___ Measuring temperature with Celsius and Fahrenheit thermometers
___ Identifying freezing and boiling points on Celsius and Fahrenheit thermometers
___ Comparing weights of objects
___ Measuring weights using U.S. and metric measures
___ Using scales to find distances on maps and globes
___ Using a protractor to measure angles
___ Measuring the radius and diameter of a circle
___ Finding the perimeter of a polygon
___ Finding the area of rectangles, triangles, and other polygons
___ Finding the circumference and area of a circle
___ Finding the volume of space figures
___ Finding the surface area of space figures
___ Estimating measurements
___ Adding, subtracting, multiplying, and dividing measurements

Geometry

___ Identifying circles, triangles, squares, and rectangles
___ Classifying objects by shapes
___ Identifying open and closed figures
___ Identifying and drawing points, line segments, lines, and rays
___ Identifying parallel and perpendicular lines
___ Identifying intersections of lines
___ Understanding and using the term "plane"
___ Recognizing and naming angles as acute, right, obtuse, and straight
___ Drawing angles
___ Identifying similar and congruent shapes
___ Identifying congruent angles
___ Identifying parts of a circle: radius, diameter, center, arc, chord, and tangent
___ Using a compass to draw circles
___ Constructing parallel and perpendicular lines

___ Constructing a bisector of a line segment and an angle
___ Identifying space figures: cubes, prisms, pyramids, cones, cylinders, and spheres
___ Naming and counting faces, edges, and vertices of space figures
___ Drawing space figures
___ Identifying symmetrical figures
___ Recognizing and drawing the slide, flip and turn of a figure

Graphing
___ Reading and making pictographs and bar, circle, and line graphs
___ Locating objects and points on a grid
___ Graphing ordered pairs of integers
___ Locating positions on the earth's grid

Problem Solving
___ Using pictures and manipulatives to solve problems
___ Writing and solving equations for pictured problems
___ Solving problems using information in graphs
___ Completing number sentences corresponding to word problems
___ Writing and solving equations for word problems
___ Estimating answers to word problems
___ Selecting information that is essential for problem solving
___ Identifying nonessential information for problem solving
___ Determining the appropriate operation for problem solving
___ Choosing a method for problem solving
___ Solving word problems involving more than one step
___ Solving problems involving money
___ Solving problems involving percentages and ratio
___ Predicting outcomes
___ Creating word problems for others to solve

MATHEMATICAL SYMBOLS

$ dollars

¢ cents

∅ empty set

[ ] empty set

% percent

∏ pi

$3.\overline{21}$ repeating decimal

45° (forty-five) degrees

F Fahrenheit

C centigrade

• point

√ square root

⌒ arc

÷ divide

⌐ divide

+ add

− subtract

× multiply

• multiply

∪ union of sets

∩ intersection of sets

= is equal to

≠ is not equal to

< less than

> greater than

≥ is greater than or equal to

≤ is less than or equal to

≈ is approximately equal to

∼ is similar to

≅ is congruent to

+4 positive integer

−4 negative integer

— line segment

↔ line

→ ray

∠ angle

m∠ measure of angle

△ triangle

⊥ perpendicular

‖ parallel

5^3 exponent

WHICH MEASURE?

LENGTH

Metric System

1 centimeter (cm)	=	10 millimeters (mm)
1 decimeter (dm)	=	10 centimeters (cm)
1 meter (m)	=	10 decimeters (dm)
1 meter (m)	=	100 centimeters (cm)
1 meter (m)	=	1000 millimeters (mm)
1 decameter (dkm)	=	10 meters (m)
1 hectometer (hm)	=	100 meters (m)
1 kilometer (km)	=	100 decameters (dkm)
1 kilometer (km)	=	1000 meters (m)

U.S. System

1 foot (ft)	=	12 inches (in)
1 yard (yd)	=	36 inches (in)
1 yard (yd)	=	3 feet (ft)
1 mile (mi)	=	5280 feet (ft)
1 mile (mi)	=	1760 yards (yd)

AREA

Metric System

1 square meter (m²)	=	100 square decimeters (dm²)
1 square meter (m²)	=	10,000 square centimeters (cm²)
1 hectare (ha)	=	0.01 square kilometer (km²)
1 hectare (ha)	=	10,000 square meters (m²)
1 square kilometer (km²)	=	1,000,000 square meters (m²)
1 square kilometer (km²)	=	100 hectares (ha)

U.S. System

1 square foot (ft²)	=	114 square inches (in²)
1 square yard (yd²)	=	9 square feet (ft²)
1 square yard (yd²)	=	1296 square inches (in²)
1 acre (a)	=	4840 square yards (yd²)
1 acre (a)	=	43,560 square feet (ft²)
1 square mile (mi²)	=	640 acres (a)

VOLUME

Metric System

1 cubic decimeter (dm³)	=	0.001 cubic meter (m³)
1 cubic decimeter (dm³)	=	1000 cubic centimeters (cm³)
1 cubic decimeter (dm³)	=	1 liter (L)
1 cubic meter (m³)	=	1,000,000 cubic centimeters (cm³)
1 cubic meter (m³)	=	1000 cubic decimeters (dm³)

U.S. System

1 cubic foot (ft³)	=	1728 cubic inches (in³)
1 cubic yard (yd³)	=	27 cubic feet (ft³)
1 cubic yard (yd³)	=	46,656 cubic inches (in³)

CAPACITY

Metric System

1 teaspoon	=	5 milliliters (mL)
1 tablespoon	=	12.5 milliliters (mL)
1 liter (L)	=	1000 milliliters (mL)
1 liter (L)	=	1000 cubic centimeters (cm³)
1 liter (L)	=	1 cubic decimeter (dm³)
1 liter (L)	=	4 metric cups
1 kiloliter (kL)	=	1000 liters (L)

U.S. System

1 tablespoon (T)	=	3 teaspoons (t)
1 cup (c)	=	16 tablespoons (T)
1 cup (c)	=	8 fluid ounces (fl oz)
1 pint (pt)	=	2 cups (c)
1 pint (pt)	=	16 fluid ounces (fl oz)
1 quart (qt)	=	4 cups (c)
1 quart (qt)	=	2 pints (pt)
1 quart (qt)	=	32 fluid ounces (fl oz)
1 gallon (gal)	=	16 cups (c)
1 gallon (gal)	=	8 pints (pt)
1 gallon (gal)	=	4 quarts (qt)
1 gallon (gal)	=	128 fluid ounces (fl oz)

─────────────── **WEIGHT** ───────────────

Metric System			**U.S. System**		
1 gram (g)	=	1000 milligrams (mg)	1 pound (lb)	=	16 ounces (oz)
1 kilogram (kg)	=	1000 grams (g)	1 ton (T)	=	2000 pounds (lb)
1 metric ton (t)	=	1000 kilograms (kg)			

─────────────── **TIME** ───────────────

1 minute (min)	=	60 seconds (sec)	1 year (yr)	=	52 weeks
1 hour (hr)	=	60 minutes (min)	1 year (yr)	=	365¼ days
1 day	=	24 hours (hr)	1 decade	=	10 years
1 week	=	7 days	1 century	=	100 years

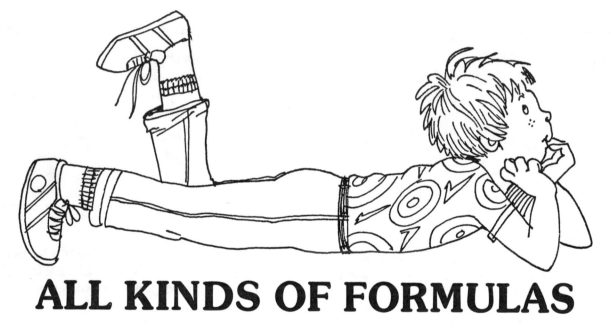

ALL KINDS OF FORMULAS

Perimeter
$P = a + b + c$ Perimeter of a triangle
$P = 2(h + w)$ Perimeter of a rectangle
$C = 2\pi r$ Circumference of a circle

Area
$A = \pi r^2$ Area of a circle
$A = s^2$ Area of a square
$A = \frac{1}{2} bh$ Area of a triangle
$A = h \dfrac{(b_1 + b_2)}{2}$ Area of a trapezoid

Volume
$V = Bh$ Volume of a rectangular
(B is area of base)   or triangular prism
$V = \frac{1}{3} Bh$ Volume of a pyramid
(B is area of base)
$V = s^3$ Volume of a cube
$V = \pi r^2 h$ Volume of a cylinder
$V = \frac{1}{3} \pi r^2 h$ Volume of a cone
$V = \frac{4}{3} \pi r^3$ Volume of a sphere

COMPUTER TALK

Basic - (Beginner's All-purpose Symbolic Instruction Code) a procedure-oriented computer programming language

Binary - a numbering system based on 2s that uses only two digits, 0 and 1; computers operate on a binary number system

Bit - one electrical signal (or one space that equals no signal) that combines with other bits to make computer codes; a binary digit

Bug - an error in the coding of a computer program

Byte - a term that measures binary digits; 8 or 16 bits

Chip - a tiny electronic component containing thousands of circuits

Cobol - (COmmon Business Oriented Language) a computer programming language

Computer - an electronic machine which stores instructions and information, deciphers and processes the instructions and information, performs tasks or calculations, and displays the "results" on a screen.

CPU - (Central Processing Unit) the part of the computer that performs logical processes

Data - information put into or received from a computer

Debug - to find and correct errors in a computer program

Disk - a thin, flat, circular metal plate with magnetic material on both sides used to store and read data

Disk Drive - a device in or attached to the computer which reads the information from the disks and stores the information

Floppy Disk - a flexible disk

Fortran - (FORmula TRANslator) a computer programming language used predominantly in science and engineering

Hard Disk - an inflexible disk

Hardware - computer machinery (such as the keyboard, disk drives, monitor, printer, and device containing the CPU)

Input - to enter data and instructions into a computer either manually or with computer input devices other than a keyboard

Interface - a connection between two computer systems or computer devices (such as the keyboard and the monitor or the printer and the computer)

Keyboard - a typewriter-like device with rows of keys which is used to type information into the computer

Memory - a device into which information can be stored

Microcomputer - a small, inexpensive computer system usually used in homes, schools, and small businesses

Monitor - a television screen which displays information

Output - information a computer displays on a screen or prints out after following a set of instructions or completing a task; information stored in memory or a computer file

Pascal - a computer programming language that emphasizes structured programming

PC - a personal computer, usually a microcomputer

Printer - a machine for printing output

Program - instructions given to a computer

Programmer - a person who prepares computer programs

RAM - (Random Access Memory) the part of a computer's memory that stores information needed for the computer to work properly (not available to the user)

Software - computer programs, usually found on disks, tapes, or cards

Terminal - a device for displaying input and output, usually located separately from the computer itself and generally consisting of a keyboard and monitor

MATH TERMS FOR EVERY OCCASION

Addend - a number being added in an addition problem

In the equation 4 + 7 = 11, 4 and 7 are addends.

Addition - an operation combining two or more numbers

Additive Inverse - for a given number, the number that can be added to give a sum of 0

-4 is the additive inverse of + 4 because - 4 + (+4) = 0

Adjacent Angle - angles that have the same vertex and a common side between them

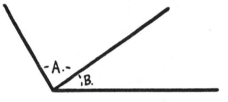

Angle A is adjacent to angle B.

Adjacent Side - the leg next to the given angle in a right triangle

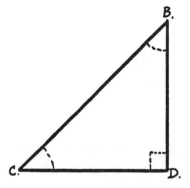

Side $\overline{CD}$ is adjacent to angle C.

Altitude of a Triangle - the distance between a point on the base and the vertex of the opposite angle, measured along a line which is perpendicular to the base (the altitude is also referred to as the height of the triangle)

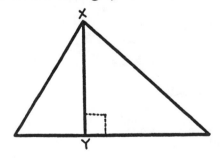

Segment $\overline{XY}$ is the altitude in this triangle.

Angle - a figure formed by two rays having a common endpoint (vertex)

An *acute angle* measures less than 90° (see # 1).

A *right angle* measures 90° (see # 2).

An *obtuse angle* measures more than 90° and less than 180° (See # 3).

A *straight angle* measures 180° (See # 4).

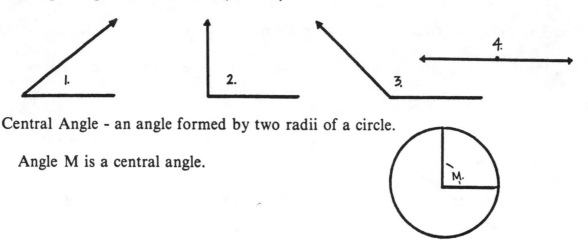

Central Angle - an angle formed by two radii of a circle.

Angle M is a central angle.

Complementary Angles - two angles whose combined measures equal 90°; X and Y (below) are complementary angles

Congruent Angles - angles having the same measure

Corresponding Angles - angles which are formed when a line intersects two parallel lines; corresponding angles are congruent; B and F (below) are corresponding angles

Supplementary Angles - two angles whose combined measures equal 180°; A and B (below) are supplementary angles

Vertical Angles - angles which are formed opposite one another when two lines intersect; vertical angles are congruent; E and H (below) are vertical angles

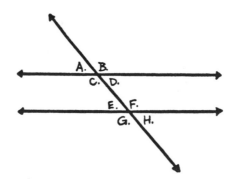

Arc - a part of a circle between any two points on the circle

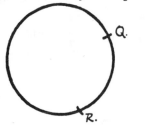

Segment $\overarc{QR}$ is an arc.

Area - the measure of the region inside a closed plane figure; area is measured in square units

Associative Property For Addition and Multiplication - the rule stating that the grouping of addends or factors does not affect the sum or product

$(3 + 6) + 9 = 3 + (6 + 9)$ $\qquad\qquad\qquad$ $(2 \times 4) \times 7 = 2 \times (4 \times 7)$

Average - the sum of a set of numbers divided by the number of addends

The average of 1, 2, 7, 3, 8, and $9 = \dfrac{1 + 2 + 7 + 3 + 8 + 9}{6} = 5$

Axes - two perpendicular number lines with a common origin

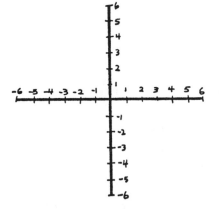

Axis - a number line which may be vertical or horizontal

Base - 1. a side of a geometric figure 2. a standard grouping of a numeration system

If a numeration system groups objects by fives, it is called a base 5 system (23 is a base 5 numeral meaning two fives and three ones).

Bisect - to divide into two congruent parts

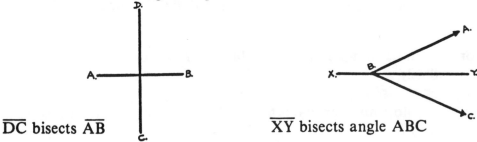

$\overline{DC}$ bisects $\overline{AB}$ $\qquad\qquad\qquad$ $\overline{XY}$ bisects angle ABC

Bisector - a line or ray that divides a segment or angle into two congruent parts

Capacity - the measure of the amount that a container will hold

Chance - the probability or likelihood of an occurrence

Chord - a line segment having endpoints on a circle

$\overline{XY}$ is a chord.

Circle - a closed curve in which all points on the edge are equidistant from a given point in the same plane

Circumference - the distance around a circle

circumference = π x diameter

Closed figure - a set of points that encloses a region in the same plane; a curve that begins and ends at the same point

Coefficient - in the expression 8x, 8 is the coefficient of x

Coincide - two lines coincide when they intersect at more than one point

Collinear - when points are on the same line, they are collinear

Common Denominator - a whole number that is the denominator for both members of a pair of fractions

For $\frac{3}{7}$ and $\frac{5}{7}$, 7 is a common denominator.

Common Factor - a whole number which is a factor of two or more numbers (3 is a factor common to 6, 9, and 12)

Common Multiple - a whole number that is a multiple of two or more numbers (12 is a multiple common to 2, 3, 4, and 6)

Commutative Property for Addition and Multiplication - the rule stating that the order of addends or factors has no effect on the sum or product

$$3 + 9 = 9 + 3 \text{ and } 4 \times 7 = 7 \times 4$$

Compass - a tool for drawing circles

Composite Number - a number having at least one whole number factor other than 1 and itself

Cone - a space figure with a circular base and a vertex

Congruent - of equal size and shape; the symbol $\cong$ means congruent

Triangles ABC and
DEF are congruent.

Coordinate Plane - a grid on a plane with two perpendicular lines of axes

Coordinates - a pair of numbers which give the location of a point on a plane

Cross Product Method - means of testing for equivalent fractions

$$\text{If } \frac{3}{5} = \frac{6}{10}, \text{ then } 3 \times 10 \text{ will equal } 5 \times 6.$$

Cube - a space figure having six congruent, square faces

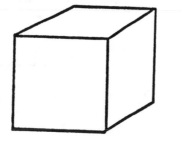

Curve - a set of points connected by a line segment

Customary Units - units of the measurement system commonly used in a given country (inches, feet, pounds, ounces, and miles are customary units in the U.S.)

Cylinder - a space figure having two congruent, circular bases

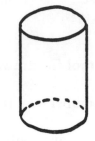

Data - figures, facts or information

Decagon - a ten-sided polygon

Decimal Numeral - a name for a fractional number expressed with a decimal point, such as .27 (4.03 is a mixed decimal)

Decimal System - a numeration system based on grouping by tens

Degree - 1. a unit of measure used in measuring angles (a circle contains 360 degrees) 2. a unit for measuring temperature

Denominator - the bottom number in a fraction; the denominator tells how many parts there are in a whole unit

Diagonal - a line segment joining two nonadjacent vertices in a polygon

$\overline{AC}$ is a diagonal in this figure.

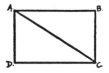

Diameter - a line segment which has its endpoints on a circle and which passes through the center of the circle

$\overline{LM}$ is the diameter of this circle.

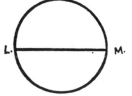

Difference - 1. the distance between two numbers on the number line 2. the result of subtracting the lesser from the greater

Digit - a symbol used to write numerals; in the decimal system, there are ten digits (0-9)

Distributive Property for Multiplication Over Addition - the rule stating that when the sum of two or more addends is multiplied by another number, each addend must be multiplied separately and then the products must be added together

$$3 \times (4 + 6 + 9) = (3 \times 4) + (3 \times 6) + (3 \times 9)$$

Dividend - a number which is to be divided in a division problem

In the equation $7\overline{)63}$, 63 is the dividend.

Divisibility - a number is divisible by a given number if the quotient of the two numbers is a whole number

189 is divisible by 9 because $189 \div 9$ is a whole number.

Division - the operation of finding a missing factor when the product and one factor are known

Divisor - the factor used in a division problem for the purpose of finding the missing factor

$$12\overline{)24}^{\,2}$$ The divisor is 12.

Elements - the members of a set

Empty Set - a set having no elements also called a null set

$\{\ \}$ or $\emptyset$ represents an empty set.

Endpoint - a point at the end of a line segment or ray

G is the endpoint of
this ray.

Equation - a mathematical sentence which states that two expressions are equal

$$7 \times 9 = 3 + (4 \times 15)$$

Equator - an imaginary line at 0 degrees latitude on the earth's grid

Equilateral - having sides of the same length

Figure ABC is an equilateral triangle. All of its sides are the same length.

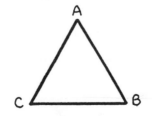

Equivalent Fractions - fractions that name the same fractional number

$$\frac{3}{4} \text{ and } \frac{9}{12} \text{ are equivalent.}$$

Equivalent Sets - sets having the same number of members

Estimate - an approximation or rough calculation

Even Number - one of the set of whole numbers having the number 2 as a factor

Expanded Notation - the method of writing a numeral to show the value of each digit

$$5327 = 5000 + 300 + 20 + 7$$

Exponent - a numeral telling how many times a number is to be used as a factor

In 6^3, the exponent is 3. $6^3 = 6 \times 6 \times 6 = 216$

Face - a plane region serving as a side of a space figure

Factor - one of two or more numbers that can be multiplied to find a product

In the equation $6 \times 9 = 54$, 6 and 9 are factors.

Factor Tree - a pictorial means of showing the factors of a number

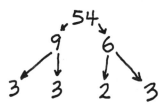

Flip - to "turn over" a geometric figure; the size or shape of the figure does not change

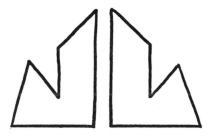

Fraction - the name for a fractional number written in the form $\frac{a}{b}$; a is the numerator, b is the denominator

Fractional Number - a number that can be named as a fraction, $\frac{a}{b}$; the numerator and denominator can be any numbers with the exception that the denominator cannot be 0

Geometry - the study of space and figures in space

Gram - a standard unit for measuring weight in the metric system

Graph - a drawing showing relationships between sets of numbers

Greatest Common Factor - the largest number that is a factor of two other numbers (6 is the greatest common factor of 18 and 24)

Grid - a set of horizontal and vertical lines spaced uniformly

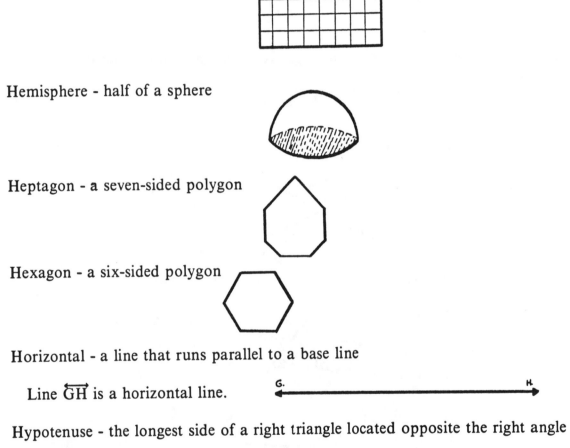

Hemisphere - half of a sphere

Heptagon - a seven-sided polygon

Hexagon - a six-sided polygon

Horizontal - a line that runs parallel to a base line

Line $\overset{\leftrightarrow}{GH}$ is a horizontal line.

Hypotenuse - the longest side of a right triangle located opposite the right angle

Side $\overline{OP}$ is the hypotenuse of this triangle.

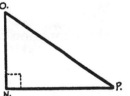

Identity Element For Addition - 0 is the identity element for addition because any number plus 0 equals that number

$$(3 + 0 = 3)$$

Identity Element For Multiplication - the number 1 is the identity element for multiplication because any number multiplied by 1 equals that number

$$(17 \times 1 = 17)$$

Improper Fraction - a fraction having a numerator equal to or greater than the denominator, therefore naming a number of 1 or more

$$\frac{9}{4} \text{ is an improper fraction.}$$

Inequality - a number sentence showing that two groups of numbers stand for different numbers

The signs $\neq$, $<$, and $>$ show inequality. $7 + 5 \neq 12 - 9$

Infinite Set - a set having an unlimited number of members

Integer - any member of the set of positive or negative counting numbers and 0

$$(. . . -4, -3, -2, -1, 0, 1, 2, 3, 4, . . .)$$

Intersection of Lines - the point at which two lines meet

Lines $\overleftrightarrow{AB}$ and $\overleftrightarrow{CD}$ intersect at point Y.

Intersection of Planes - a line formed by the set of points at which two planes meet

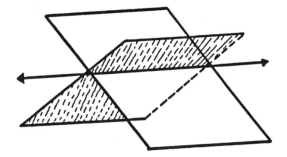

Intersection of Sets - the set of members common to each of two or more sets

The intersection of these sets is 3, 7, and 8. The symbol $\cap$ represents intersection.

Inverse - opposite; addition and subtraction are inverse operations and multiplication is the inverse of division

226

Latitude - the distance, measured in degrees, north or south of the equator; lines of latitude run parallel to the equator

Least Common Denominator - the smallest whole number which is a multiple of the denominators of two or more fractions

The least common denominator for $\frac{1}{3}$ and $\frac{3}{4}$ is 12.

Least Common Multiple - the smallest whole number which is divisible by each of two or more given numbers

The least common multiple of 2, 6, 9, and 18 is 18.

Legs - sides adjacent to the right angle in a right triangle

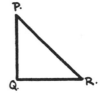

$\overline{QP}$ and $\overline{QR}$ are legs
in this triangle.

Like Fractions - fractions having the same denominator

$\frac{2}{9}$ and $\frac{12}{9}$ are like fractions.

Line - one of the four undefined terms of geometry used to define all other terms

Line of Symmetry - a line on which a figure can be folded so that the two parts are exactly the same

Line $\overleftrightarrow{ST}$ is the line of
symmetry in this figure.

Line Segment - part of a line consisting of a path between two endpoints

$\overline{AB}$ and $\overline{CD}$ are line segments.

Linear Measure (or length) - the measure of distance between two points along a line

Liter - a metric system unit of measurement for liquid capacity

Longitude - the distance, measured in degrees, east or west of the prime meridian; lines of longitude run north and south on the earth's grid, meeting at the poles

Lowest Terms - when a fraction has a numerator and denominator with no common factor greater than 1, the fraction is in lowest terms

$$\frac{3}{7} \text{ is a fraction in lowest terms.}$$

Mean - average; the sum of numbers in a set divided by the number of addends

The mean of 6, 8, 9, 19, and 38 is $\frac{80}{5}$ or 16.

Measurement - the process of finding the length, area, capacity, or amount of something

Median - the middle number in a set of numbers; the median is determined by arranging numbers in order from lowest to highest and by counting to the middle

The median of (3, 8, 12, 17, 20, 23, 27) is 17.

Meter - a metric system unit of linear measurement

Metric System - a system of measurement based on the decimal system

Midpoint - a point that divides a line segment into two congruent segments

Point B is the midpoint
of DE.

D. _____ B. _____ E.

Mixed Numeral - a numeral that includes a whole number and a fractional number or a whole number and a decimal

$$7\frac{1}{2} \text{ and } 37.016 \text{ are mixed numerals.}$$

Multiple - the product of two whole numbers

Multiplication - an operation involving repeated addition

$$4 \times 5 = 4 + 4 + 4 + 4 + 4$$

Multiplicative Inverse - for any given number, the number that will yield a product of 1

$\frac{4}{3}$ is the multiplicative inverse of $\frac{3}{4}$ because $\frac{4}{3} \times \frac{3}{4} = 1$.

Negative Integer - one of a set of counting numbers that is less than 0

Nonagon - a nine-sided polygon

Number - a mathematical idea concerning the amount contained in a set

Number Line - a line which has numbers corresponding to points along it

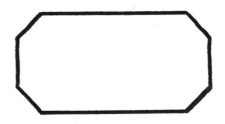

Numeral - a symbol used to represent or name a number

Numeration System - a system of symbols used to express numbers

Numerator - the number above the line in a fraction

Octagon - an eight-sided polygon

Odd Number - a whole number belonging to the set of numbers equal to (n x 2) + 1

(1, 3, 5, 7, 9 . . .) are odd numbers.

Odds Against - the ratio of the number of unfavorable outcomes to the number of favorable outcomes

Odds in Favor - the ratio of the number of favorable outcomes to the number of unfavorable outcomes

Opposite Property - a property which states that if the sum of two numbers is 0, then each number is the opposite of the other

-4 + 4 = 0 ; -4 and 4 are opposites

Ordered Pair - a pair of numbers in a certain order with the order being of significance

Ordinal Number - a number telling the place of an item in an ordered set (sixth, eighth, etc.)

Origin - the beginning point on a number line; the origin is often 0

Outcome - a possible result in a probability experiment

Palindrome - a number which reads the same forward and backward

(343, 87678, 91219, etc.)

Parallel Lines - lines in the same plane which do not intersect

These lines
are parallel.

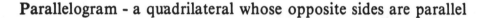

Parallelogram - a quadrilateral whose opposite sides are parallel

Pentagon - a five-sided polygon

Percent - a comparison of a number with 100

43 compared to 100 is 43%

Perimeter - the distance around the outside of a closed figure

Periods - groups of three digits in numbers

723,301,611

millions period   thousands period   units period

Perpendicular Lines - two lines in the same plane that intersect at right angles

These lines are
perpendicular to
one another.

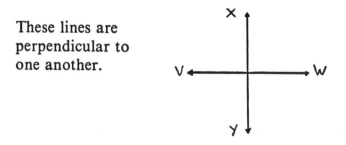

Pi - the ratio of a circle's circumference to its diameter

pi = 3.14159265 (a non-terminating decimal)

The symbol π signifies pi.

Pictograph - a graph that uses pictures or symbols to represent numbers

Place Value - the value assigned to a digit due to its position in a numeral

Plane - the set of all points on a flat surface which extends indefinitely in all directions

Plane Figure - a set of points in the same plane enclosing a region

Figures A and B are plane figures.

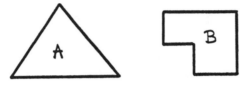

Point - one of the four undefined terms in geometry used to define all other terms

Polygon - a simple, closed plane figure having line segments as sides

Polyhedron - a space figure formed by intersecting plane surfaces called faces

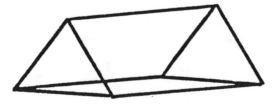

Positive Integer - one of a set of counting numbers that is greater than 0

Prime Factor - a factor that is a prime number

1, 2, and 5 are prime factors of 20

Prime Number - a number whose only number factors are 1 and itself

Prism - a space figure with two parallel, congruent polygonal faces (called bases); a prism is named by the shape of its bases

triangular prism   rectangular prism

Probability - a study of the likelihood that an event will occur

Product - the answer in a multiplication problem

Property of One - a property which states that any number multiplied by 1 will equal that number

Property of Zero - a property which states that any number plus zero equals that number

Proportion - a number statement of equality between two ratios

$$\frac{3}{7} = \frac{9}{21}$$

Protractor - an instrument used for measuring angles

Pyramid - a space figure having one polygonal base and four triangular faces which have a common vertex

Quadrilateral - a four-sided polygon

Quotient - the answer in a division problem

Radius - a line segment having one endpoint in the center of the circle and another on the circle

$\overline{FG}$ is the radius of
this circle.

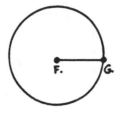

Rate - a comparison of two quantities

Ratio - a comparison of two numbers expressed as $\dfrac{a}{b}$

Ray - a portion of a line extending from one endpoint in one direction indefinitely

Reciprocal Method For Dividing Fractions - a means of dividing fractions that involves replacing the divisor with its reciprocal and then multiplying

$$\frac{2}{3} \div \frac{4}{7} = \frac{2}{3} \times \frac{7}{4} = \frac{14}{12} = 1\frac{1}{6}$$

Reciprocals - a pair of numbers whose product is one

$\frac{1}{2}$ and $\frac{2}{1}$ are reciprocals.

Rectangle - a parallelogram having four right angles

Region - the set of all points on a closed curve and in its interior

Remainder - the number (less than the divisor) that is left after a division problem is completed

$$\begin{array}{r} 20 \\ 21\overline{)426} \quad\quad 6 = \text{remainder} \\ 420 \\ \hline 6 \end{array}$$

Rename - to name numbers with a different set of numerals

Repeating Decimal - a decimal in which a certain set of digits repeats without end (0.363636)

Rhombus - a parallelogram having congruent sides

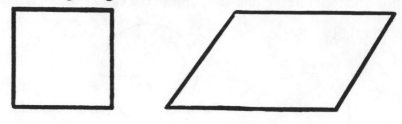

Roman Numerals - numerals used by the Romans for keeping records

Rounding - disregarding all digits in a number beyond a certain significance

Scale Drawing - a drawing of an object with all distances in proportion to the corresponding distances on the actual object

Scientific Notation - a number expressed as a decimal number (usually with an absolute value less than 10) multiplied by a power of 10.

$$4.53 \times 10^3 = 4530$$

Segment - two points and all of the points on the line or arc between them

Sequence - a continuous series of numbers ordered according to a pattern

Set - a collection of items called members or elements

Similarity - a property of geometric figures having angles of the same size

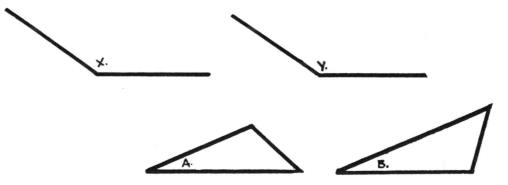

Angles X and Y are similar.   Triangles A and B are similar.

Simple Closed Curve or Figure - a closed curve whose path does not intersect itself

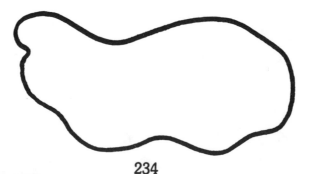

Skip Count - counting by skipping a certain number of digits (counting by 2s, 5s, and 10s, etc.)

Slide - moving a figure without turning or flipping it; the shape or size of a figure is not changed by a slide

Solution - the number that replaces a variable to complete an equation

Solution Set - the set of possible solutions for a number sentence

Space Figure - a figure which consists of a set of points in two or more planes

Sphere - a space figure formed by a set of points equidistant from a center point

Square - a rectangle with congruent sides

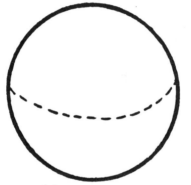

Statistics - numerical observations or data

Subset - every member of a set, or any combination of the members of a set

Subtraction - the operation of finding a missing addend when one addend and the sum are known

Sum - the answer in an addition problem resulting from the combination of two addends

Surface - a region lying on one plane

Surface Area - the space covered by a plane region or by the faces of a space figure

Symmetric Figure - a figure having two halves that are reflections of one another; a line of symmetry divides the figure into two congruent parts

These figures
are symmetric.

Tangent - a line which touches a curve at only one point

Line $\overleftrightarrow{GH}$ is tangent to the
circle at point X.

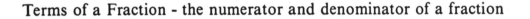

Terms of a Fraction - the numerator and denominator of a fraction

Transversal - a line that intersects two or more parallel lines

$\overleftrightarrow{GH}$ is a transversal of
lines $\overleftrightarrow{AB}$ and $\overleftrightarrow{CD}$.

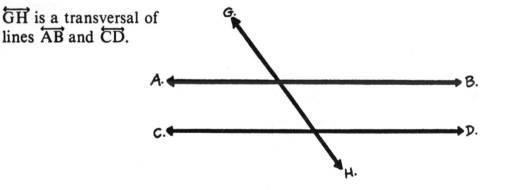

Trapezoid - a quadrilateral having only two parallel sides

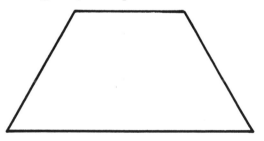

Triangle - a three-sided polygon

Acute Triangle - a triangle in which all three angles are less than 90°

Equilateral Triangle - a triangle with three congruent sides and three congruent angles

Isosceles Triangle - a triangle with at least two congruent sides

Obtuse Triangle - a triangle having one angle greater than 90°

Right Triangle - a triangle having one 90° angle

Scalene Triangle - a triangle in which no two sides are congruent

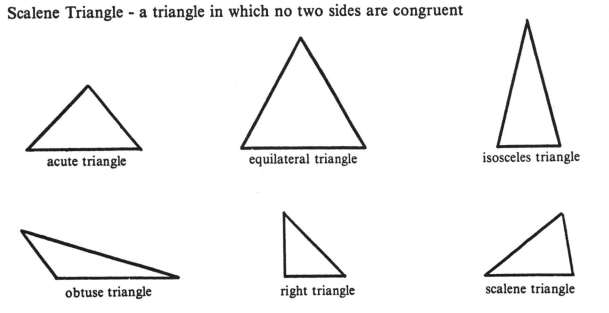

acute triangle   equilateral triangle   isosceles triangle

obtuse triangle   right triangle   scalene triangle

Turn - a move in geometry which involves turning, but not flipping, a figure; the size or shape of a figure is not changed by a turn

Union of Sets - a set containing the combined members of two or more sets; the symbol ∪ represents union

The union of sets
A and B is
(7, 12, 14, 20, 26, and 25).

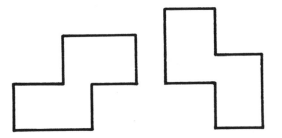

Unit - 1. the first whole number 2. a determined quantity used as a standard for measurement

Venn Diagram - a pictorial means of representing sets and the union or intersection of sets (see example under Union of Sets)

Vertex - a common endpoint of two rays forming an angle, two line segments forming sides of a polygon, or two planes forming a polyhedron

Point Z is the vertex
of this angle.

Vertical - a line that is perpendicular to a horizontal base line

Line $\overleftrightarrow{KL}$ is vertical.

Volume - the measure of capacity or space enclosed by a space figure

Whole Number - a member of the set of numbers (0, 1, 2, 3, 4 . . .)

X-Axis - the horizontal number line on a coordinate grid

Y-Axis - the vertical number line on a coordinate grid

Zero - the number of members in an empty set

Pg. 16   1) 10, 12, 14, 16   2) 15, 20, 25, 30   3) 30, 40, 50, 60, 70   4) 12, 15, 18, 21

Pg. 23   1) 8   2) 1500   3) 61   4) 103   5) 157   6) 19   7) 39   8) 580   9) 111

Pg. 33   1) 586   2) 190   3)208   4)583   5)863   6) 960   7) 247   8) 900   9) 929

Pg. 49   1) 26   2) 0   3) 100   4) 28   5) 100   6) 33   7) 30   8) 59

Pg. 51   1) no   2) yes   3)

6	9	6
7	7	7
8	5	8

4)

4	9	2
3	5	7
8	1	6

Pg. 52   1)

5	10	3
4	6	8
9	2	7

2)

8	3	10
9	7	5
4	11	6

3) no   4) no

5)

9	4	11
10	8	6
5	12	7

6)

9	14	7
8	10	12
13	6	11

Pg. 53   20 minutes

Pg. 55   8000 feet

Pg. 57   A. 1)> 2)> 3)> 4)< 5)< 6)< 7)> 8)<   B. 1)< 2)< 3)< 4)<

Pg. 59   1) 15   2) 41   3) 16   4) 21   5) 10   6) 12

Pg. 60   A) 70   B) 300   C) 70   D) 110   E) 300   F) 500

Pg. 66-   1) 9-zebra   2) 4-seal   3) 6-bear   4) 8-camel   5) 7-lion   6) 3-elephant
67   7) 5-kangaroo   8) 2-giraffe   9) 10-poodle

Pg. 69   1) 13 x 6 = 78 miles   2) 9 x 18 = 162 miles   3) 25 ÷ 5 = 5 hours
4) 3 x 15 = 45 miles, 7 x 4 = 28 miles; John went farther.

Pg. 75   1) 99   2) 53   3) 666   4) 25   5) 12   6) 50   7) 100   8) 28   9) 511   10) 75   11) 411   12) 41

Pg. 79

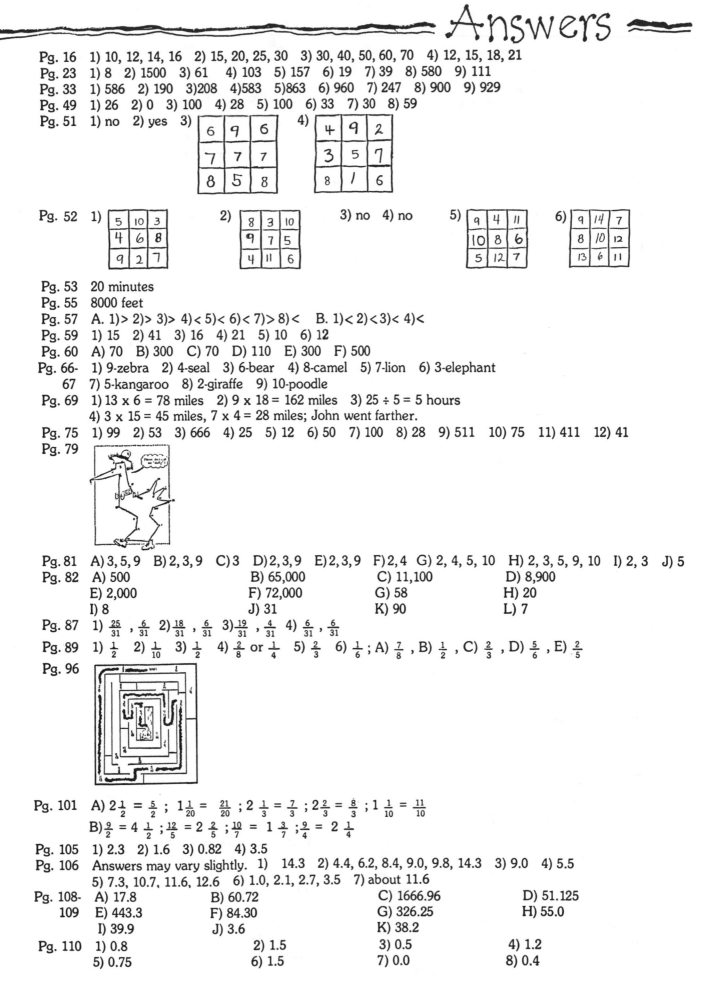

Pg. 81   A) 3, 5, 9   B) 2, 3, 9   C) 3   D) 2, 3, 9   E) 2, 3, 9   F) 2, 4   G) 2, 4, 5, 10   H) 2, 3, 5, 9, 10   I) 2, 3   J) 5

Pg. 82   A) 500   B) 65,000   C) 11,100   D) 8,900
E) 2,000   F) 72,000   G) 58   H) 20
I) 8   J) 31   K) 90   L) 7

Pg. 87   1) $\frac{25}{31}$, $\frac{6}{31}$ 2)$\frac{18}{31}$, $\frac{6}{31}$ 3)$\frac{19}{31}$, $\frac{4}{31}$ 4) $\frac{6}{31}$, $\frac{6}{31}$

Pg. 89   1) $\frac{1}{2}$ 2) $\frac{1}{10}$ 3) $\frac{1}{2}$ 4) $\frac{2}{8}$ or $\frac{1}{4}$ 5) $\frac{2}{3}$ 6) $\frac{1}{6}$; A) $\frac{7}{8}$, B) $\frac{1}{2}$, C) $\frac{2}{3}$, D) $\frac{5}{6}$, E) $\frac{2}{5}$

Pg. 96

Pg. 101   A) $2\frac{1}{2} = \frac{5}{2}$; $1\frac{1}{20} = \frac{21}{20}$; $2\frac{1}{3} = \frac{7}{3}$; $2\frac{2}{3} = \frac{8}{3}$; $1\frac{1}{10} = \frac{11}{10}$
B)$\frac{9}{2} = 4\frac{1}{2}$; $\frac{12}{5} = 2\frac{2}{5}$; $\frac{10}{7} = 1\frac{3}{7}$; $\frac{9}{4} = 2\frac{1}{4}$

Pg. 105   1) 2.3   2) 1.6   3) 0.82   4) 3.5

Pg. 106   Answers may vary slightly.   1)   14.3   2) 4.4, 6.2, 8.4, 9.0, 9.8, 14.3   3) 9.0   4) 5.5
5) 7.3, 10.7, 11.6, 12.6   6) 1.0, 2.1, 2.7, 3.5   7) about 11.6

Pg. 108-   A) 17.8   B) 60.72   C) 1666.96   D) 51.125
109   E) 443.3   F) 84.30   G) 326.25   H) 55.0
I) 39.9   J) 3.6   K) 38.2

Pg. 110   1) 0.8   2) 1.5   3) 0.5   4) 1.2
5) 0.75   6) 1.5   7) 0.0   8) 0.4

Pg. 116 1) A 2) 0 3) R 4) A 5) A 6) 0 7) R 8) R

Pg. 117 1) 3   2) 4   3) 8   4) 5   5) 2   6) 1
7) 4   8) 0   9) 3   10) 2   11) 0   12) 2
13) 0   14 2   15) 1   16) 4

Pg. 129 1) no 2) yes 3) no 4) yes 5) no 6) yes 7) yes 8) yes

Pg. 131 1) C 2) B 3) D 4) C

Pg. 132 1) C 2) B 3) D 4) D

Pg. 142 Answers may vary slightly.
1) 18 cm 2) 14 cm 3) 14 cm 4) 14 cm 5) 10 cm 6) 22 cm 7) 18 cm 8) 10 cm

Pg. 143 Answers may vary slightly.
1) 21 m 2) 30 m 3) 28 m 4) 24 m 5) 23 m

Pg. 145 1) 12 cm² 2) 20 cm² 3) 14 cm² 4) 17 cm²

Pg. 146 A) 24 cm² B) 16 cm² C) 18 cm² D) 16 cm² E) 26 cm²

Pg. 147 1) 15 m² 2) 32 m² 3) 21 m² 4) 18 m²

Pg. 151 A) 5 B) 3 C) 1 D) 2

Pg. 152- 1) area 2) volume 3) volume 4) length 5) area
153 6) volume 7) length 8) volume 9) length 10) length 11) volume 12) length 13) length

Pg. 155 1) g 2) kg 3) t 4) kg 5) g 6) g

Pg. 161 1) F 2) E 3) C 4) A 5) 8:00 6) 4:15 7) 2:51 8) 10:10

Pg. 164 A) 120 B) 90 C) 3 D) 600 E) $\frac{3}{4}$ hour

Pg. 165 Missy Mouse - $ .85; Molly Moo $18.00; Harry Hound - $ 7.30; Brian Bear - $11.90

Pg. 168 Bertha

Pg. 173 K - 30; 1st - 30; 2nd - 40; 3rd - 70; 4th - 70; 5th - 90

Pg. 176 1) Maria; Andy 2) Nancy & Maria 3) Donny 4) Yo 5) 180

Pg. 177 1) 22 2) 20 3) Teresa 4) Tuesday 5) Monday 6) Thursday 7) 10

Pg. 178 1) reading 2) math, art, reading 3) art 4) spelling 5) 6 hours

Pg. 180 1) (1,1) 2) robot 3) kite 4) (4,2) 5) (2,4) 6) glove 7) (7,0) 8) (3,3)

Pg. 181 Secret Message: You are a super kid!

Pg. 182 1) (1,1) 2) (2, -4) 3) ant 4) (-4, -2) 5) cupcake 6) (0, 4)

Pg. 184 (-1, -3)

Pg. 186 1, 3, 5

Pg. 187 1) 246 ÷ 6 = 41 2) 2 + 3 = 5 3) 2 x 5 = 10

Pg. 188- 1) Date   2) Plum   3) Fig   4) Fig   5) Date
189 6) Plum   7) Plum   8) Fig   9) Date   10) Nut

Pg. 191

Pg. 193 Hidden picture: an airplane

Pg. 197 1) $\frac{1}{12}$ 2) $\frac{6}{12}$ or $\frac{1}{2}$ 3) $\frac{6}{12}$ or $\frac{1}{2}$ 4) $\frac{2}{12}$ or $\frac{1}{6}$ 5) $\frac{4}{12}$ or $\frac{1}{3}$
6) $\frac{3}{12}$ or $\frac{1}{4}$ 7) $\frac{4}{12}$ or $\frac{1}{3}$ 8) $\frac{7}{12}$ 9) $\frac{5}{12}$ 10) $\frac{8}{12}$ or $\frac{2}{3}$

Pg. 198 1) how many other socks there are
2) a question
3) how many rooms are not bedrooms
4) a question
5) the amount of time Wally looked for socks during the rest of the week
6) how old Wally is now

Pg. 199 1) Sam 2) about 50 meters 3) Sasha 4) about 70 meters 5) no
6) across the street and through Julie's backyard 7) Jason — about 150 meters;
Craig — about 120 meters

Pg. 200 1) Shakers 2) Shakers 3) Shakers 93, Stompers 85

Pg. 201 A) 2519 miles B) 850 miles C) 50 miles D) 2923 miles

Pg. 203 1) $37.06 2) $14.39 3) 49 minutes 4) 11 minutes
5) Steven's dad — $3.67 more 6) $6.05